A Very Pink Wedding

A GAY GUIDE TO PLANNING YOUR PERFECT DAY

NICOLA HILL

Collins

Dedicated to Laura McCaffrey
for the love, support and encouragement
she has given me while writing this book
and in our lives together.

First published in 2007 by Collins,
an imprint of HarperCollins Publishers Ltd
77–85 Fulham Palace Road
London W6 8JB

The Collins website address is www.collins.co.uk

Text © 2007 Nicola Hill
Illustration © 2007 Trina Dalziel
12 11 10 09 08 07
10 9 8 7 6 5 4 3 2 1

A catalogue record for this book is available from the British Library.

ISBN 978-0-00-725742-3

Printed and bound by Martins the Printers Limited, Berwick upon Tweed

Contents

Introduction

Congratulations on taking the first steps towards planning your perfect wedding day. The fact that same-sex couples can now make a legal commitment to each other akin to marriage is fantastic. And whether you want to celebrate your civil partnership with an intimate gathering of close friends or a massive extravaganza, this book will guide you through all the possibilities. It will give you ideas for styles, themes and money-saving tips, and enable you to identify key priorities. It will guide you step-by-step through the different stages of planning your wedding, from the proposal and booking a registry office to choosing a venue, deciding on flowers and entertainment, organising speeches and setting a running order for the day. The book includes useful checklists and charts to help you set budgets, monitor quotations and make sure you have remembered all the details. There are also key questions to ask suppliers to check you are getting the best service and value for money. As well as relating some of my own experiences, I have included practical advice from wedding organisers, caterers and many other suppliers.

Organising your wedding can be a bit of an emotional roller coaster, with big decisions to make, family pressure and even stress between the two of you. The main thing is to focus on what you really want and why you are doing it. To encourage you through the planning process, I have included some thoughts and tips from gay men and lesbians who have already tied the knot. Some have had traditional weddings in morning suits and frocks, while others have had intimate ceremonies with close friends.

You may want to adapt some elements of a traditional wedding, or create your own unique style – there are no rules. Your actual wedding day will rush by in a flurry of excitement and emotion, so make sure you enjoy the build-up and have fun planning it.

My journey from straight to gay weddings

The first time I got married, I looked up weddings in the Sydney Yellow Pages, found a registrar who held ceremonies in his front room, and booked him for a month later. I was 24 and marrying my Australian boyfriend in high dudgeon, as this was the only way we could live together in England. We wanted to be together, but wouldn't have bothered to marry if English law had recognised our unmarried union.

A month later, I ironed my only frock. My mother told me I should have something borrowed, something blue, something old and something new. I borrowed a ring, wore blue pants, had an old lace hanky and new flip-flops, but that was about the only tradition we adhered to. We had two witnesses and got married in the registrar's front room. We followed it up with a slap-up meal of fish and chips with champagne in the local pub. The whole thing cost less than £100. Shortly afterwards we returned to the UK and I started working in a hotel that ran two weddings every weekend.

My first marriage lasted only a few years and, when I turned 28, I realised I preferred women. Fifteen years later, I began planning my own gay wedding.

I met Laura at a women's group in London. It turns out she was brought up in a village ten miles away from where I grew up – practically, the girl next door.

Given my experience, I was a bit wary about getting married again and hadn't wanted any commitment ceremony before the law changed. Aren't a mortgage, a shared editorial business and two toasters enough? However, when the Civil Partnership Act was passed in March 2005, I realised its significance. Gay couples can now enjoy nearly all the same rights as married straight couples and it is the first time that same-sex couples have been legally recognised in our society. It really is a monumental step forward for all gay men and lesbians.

In April 2005, for our 10th anniversary of meeting, Laura and I went on holiday to Greece. I decided to propose at the Parthenon, overlooking Athens. It seemed romantic to me. 'Laura,' I gasped, for dramatic effect. 'I've got something to ask you. Will you marry me?' Happily, she said yes.

On our return, I started researching wedding venues. Press reports at the time indicated that 30-40 per cent of hotels refused gay custom. So I was explicit in my e-mail requests, saying it was for a civil partnership ceremony and that I wanted to be reassured that I wouldn't experience any homophobia. About 35 per cent of venues didn't bother to reply and a couple of others certainly didn't seem very friendly. This set me thinking, and I woke up one Sunday morning with an idea for a new business.

Luckily, it was a Bank Holiday weekend and within two days I'd written a business plan. Laura prepared the cash-flow forecast, while I wrote the website copy and found a web developer. We then registered the domain name – gay-friendly-wedding-venues.com – and designed the front page. We launched in July 2005.

Within the first year, the website attracted over 800 advertisers, ranging from bishops to balloon companies, ships to castles. We won an award for best start-up business and a grant from an enterprise support organisation.

When the law changed in December 2005, I also ended up defending our right to marriage on national television, radio and in newspaper articles. Laura and I were even interviewed by the TV news programme 'Good Morning America' and a Korean news station.

As well as the knowledge gained from setting up the business, I am able to share my experience of planning our own wedding in this book.

I feel Laura and I grew even closer as a result of organising our wedding. We took time out to focus on what we both wanted, and learned more about each other. It was a bonding experience and felt like an enormous privilege to be living in an era when we can celebrate our love and be legally recognised. We also had a lot of fun – as well as a few nervous moments – planning such a big gathering of friends and family. In the end, it was a fabulous day and one that we will treasure forever.

I hope this book will help you to enjoy the planning stages and have a fantastic pink wedding. You deserve it!

History being made

The build-up to the change in the law in the UK began in June 2003, when the Government published a consultation document outlining its proposal to set up a civil partnership registration scheme for same-sex couples.

The responses to the consultation were summarised in a document that can be read at: www.womenandequalityunit.gov.uk/publications/CP_responses.doc.

On 30 September 2003 the Scottish Executive published a consultation paper on the devolved aspects of a civil partnership registration scheme for same-sex couples. A similar consultation exercise was carried out on proposals for a civil partnership registration scheme in Northern Ireland, in early 2004.

The Civil Partnership Act 2004 covers the whole of the UK, but takes account of the different legal frameworks in Scotland and Northern Ireland.

The Bill is published

The Government published the Civil Partnership Bill on 31 March 2004. It was then debated in both houses with various proposed amendments, one of which was to allow carers or siblings the right to have a civil partnership, but this was rejected. The Bill was passed and on 18 November 2004 it received Royal Assent. However, it took more than a year to implement the Civil Partnership Act, due in some measure to the changes needed to tax and benefits computer systems.

Changes to the tax system were made in the 2005 Finance Bill, enabling civil partners to be treated as a married couple for inheritance tax purposes. On 5 December 2005, The Civil Partnership Act 2004 was implemented – gay couples were finally able to register, and the rest, as they say, is history.

Landmark case

In the first year of the Civil Partnership Act, two British professors, Celia Kitzinger and Susan Wilkinson, took a challenge to the High Court asking for recognition of the marriage they had held in Canada, where gay marriage is treated in exactly the same way as straight. Any heterosexual couple who marries abroad automatically has their marriage recognised as a marriage in the UK. The lesbian couple claimed that by being

> 66 Civil partnership registration underlines the inherent value of committed same-sex relationships. It supports stable families and shows that we really respect the diversity of the society we live in. It opens the way to respect, recognition and justice for those who have been denied it too long. 99 Jacqui Smith MP, Minister for Equality, June 2003

viewed only as civil partners on their return to the UK, their human rights were impeded.

Had the courts agreed, we might now be using the word 'marriage' rather than the awkward phrase 'civil partnership ceremony'. Sadly, Sir Mark Potter, President of the Family Division of the High Court, ruled that their union could be recognised only as a civil partnership.

Throughout this book I have used the words marriage, wedding and civil partnership ceremony interchangeably. This is not meant to cause any offence to religious people, but these words are being used in common parlance to describe gay unions. From a writer's point of view, civil partnership ceremony is very long-winded and it would have made the book twice as long if I had used the term on every occasion.

The first ceremonies

A huge rush to register in the first few months saw the Government's conservative predictions fly out the window. The government had estimated that 11,000 couples would tie the knot in the first four years. In fact, in the first nine months 15,672 couples got hitched, with guys outnumbering girls by almost two to one. For the latest figures and more statistics, visit: www.statistics.gov.uk and search under civil partnerships.

The first civil partnership ceremonies were held in Northern Ireland, on Monday, 19 December 2005. Couples in Scotland made history a day later, and then, because of a slightly longer registration period, England and Wales caught up on the Wednesday.

The first couple to publicly

66 We could not be here without the hard work of many queer activists. We feel very privileged and blessed to be here doing this and look forward to having a wonderful day. **99** Shannon Sickels celebrate their civil partnership in the UK were Shannon Sickels, an American playwright, and Grainne Close, a community worker from County Antrim in Northern Ireland. The ceremony took place on 19 December 2005 at Belfast City Hall. Sadly, they were harangued by Evangelical protestors – but fortunately the protestors were balanced out by over 100 close friends and family and a crowd of well-wishers.

Both women wore trouser suits – Shannon in white and Grainne in black – and each had simple flowers in their lapels. They had a 30-minute ceremony and exchanged matching platinum and diamond rings.

As they were surrounded by the world's press, Grainne told reporters: 'We just want to say that this is a very privileged position we are in this morning and for us this is about making a choice.'

Grainne and Shannon left the media circus in a traditional black taxi with a yellow ribbon tied to its bonnet – classy.

My cousin, Philip Reay-Smith, who is openly gay, was covering the civil partnership story for ITV News and had to interview one of the clergymen. His report was being screened while I was sitting in ITV's newsroom in London, waiting to be grilled about the same subject – a real family affair.

The first men to celebrate their civil partnership on 19 December, in Belfast, were Henry Kane and Christopher Flanagan, who arrived at the City Hall in a very camp pink stretch limousine.

On 21 December 2005, rock legend Sir Elton John and his partner, David Furnish, became the first celebrity couple to tie the knot in England. They had been together for 13 years. After a simple ceremony at Windsor registry office, they held a lavish reception at their home nearby.

> **❝ I thought I might get the odd flour bomb, but there was no negative reaction. It was the nicest day of my life, with all the people I love most. ❞** Elton John

Elton told the *Mirror* newspaper: 'I didn't think I'd feel different [after the ceremony] but I do. I felt secure. It was the icing on the cake.' He added: 'The best thing about the whole day was the great British public.'

A year later, on 17 December 2006, *Little Britain* creator and star Matt Lucas married his boyfriend Kevin McGee in a pantomime-themed civil partnership ceremony. A civil partnership storyline was also written into the BBC Radio 4 serial *The Archers*, with Ian and Adam causing a stir in Ambridge.

Politicians pop the question

In May 2006, Labour's David Borrow became the first MP to have a civil partnership; and in June Ben Bradshaw was the first government minister to wed his long-term partner, Neal Dalgleish – a BBC Newsnight journalist.

Chris Smith, the first openly gay MP and now a Lord, married his long-term partner at a simple ceremony in Islington in July 2006,

---

David and John's private ceremony, followed by a party

My partner John and I decided to have a very simple ceremony at Preston registry office, with immediate family members invited and no publicity. Three months later, we had a party at a hotel in my constituency with family, friends and colleagues, which was great. We did not expect to feel any different after the civil partnership, but it has made us feel more secure. We are glad we did it.

David Borrow MP, South Ribble

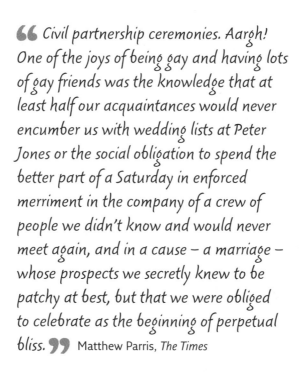

followed, a month later, by Matthew Parris, the former Conservative MP and *Times* columnist, who had jokingly lamented civil partnerships, saying they would ruin people's Saturdays.

66 *Civil partnership ceremonies. Aargh! One of the joys of being gay and having lots of gay friends was the knowledge that at least half our acquaintances would never encumber us with wedding lists at Peter Jones or the social obligation to spend the better part of a Saturday in enforced merriment in the company of a crew of people we didn't know and would never meet again, and in a cause – a marriage – whose prospects we secretly knew to be patchy at best, but that we were obliged to celebrate as the beginning of perpetual bliss.* **99** Matthew Parris, *The Times*

How to use this guide

You've taken the decision to have a civil partnership ceremony and now you want to get on with planning your big day. This guide helps you get started with wish lists, budget planners and the vital timetable. Once you start looking at venues and researching suppliers, this book gives you lots of money-saving tips and other useful advice, to ensure all will go smoothly.

If you haven't done so already, the first stage is to check you are fully aware of the legal implications of a civil partnership, and in Chapter One there is a short question and answer section on the Civil Partnership Act, including advice on where to obtain further information. It also offers information on marrying abroad.

Chapter Two takes you through popping the question, choosing engagement rings and celebrating your decision. To start you thinking about how you want to shape your big day, Chapter Two tells you how to create a wish list, to help you decide on the style of wedding you want. There's a copy of the list at the back of the book, which you should fill in and refer to throughout your wedding planning. There's also advice on how to decide who to invite and the advantages of using a wedding planner.

Budgeting

Once you have decided on the various elements of your wedding, and bearing in mind all the essentials in the Countdown timetable on pages 20-22, you should then turn to the Budget Planner, Table 2 at the back of the book (pages 218-224), and set a maximum budget for each of the items that will be contributing to your big day. There is also a section in this table where you can write down who is responsible for obtaining the various estimates. At this point, too, with your budget in place, it's a good idea to open a bank account specifically for your wedding.

Then, later, when you have selected your venues, suppliers and products and agreed prices, you can start to fill in the final column in the Budget Plan so that you can keep a tally of what you are spending. There is also an online version of this available to download at www.gay-friendly-wedding-venues.com/budget.

Countdown timetable

Many guides will tell you to plan your wedding at least a year ahead, but, bearing in mind that you must give notice at your registry office of your intention to have a civil partnership at least 15 clear days before the ceremony itself, you can take as long or as short a time as you want. This will depend on what you need, how much you are willing to spend and whether you can compromise.

The Countdown timetable on pages 20-22 is based on your having a year, but you can concertina this into a shorter period – whatever time you have allowed, divide the time up, allocate tasks to each period, and put the deadlines in your diary or wedding planner. For example, if you have only six months, divide that time into 12 two-week slots and allocate time to find suppliers, choose venues, buy outfits, etc. You will probably need to revise this as you go along, but by putting everything in your diary, nothing will be missed off the list. On the other hand, if you want to book extremely popular venues and suppliers, you will need to start even earlier than one year ahead. As regards the order of tasks given in the timetable, you can be flexible to some extent – you may want to confirm the venue before anything else, or you could buy a cake the week before from a supermarket or bakery, but this guide gives you an idea of how to prioritise your planning.

Use the Countdown timetable in conjunction with the information in the relevant chapter.

Getting organised

In Chapter Three you'll find advice on the big decisions you need to make – choosing themes and styles for your big day, finding a venue, looking at catering options, and booking and meeting the registrar. There are useful checklists, too, listing the key questions you should ask when you first contact venues and caterers, other points to bear in mind, and money-saving tips.

When these decisions have been taken, you need to spend a bit of time on administration, sorting out wedding insurance, Wills and other financial matters. You will also need to choose your stationery because you'll want to start sending out 'save the date' cards as soon as possible. But it's not all administration – included in this chapter is information on booking your honeymoon, with advice on places to choose, such as gay-friendly destinations, and other points to consider.

As you move on to booking suppliers – from photographers to musicians and florists to car hire – check out the useful advice in the next chapter on what to ask suppliers to make sure you get best value for money and an excellent service. Then, as you get final quotes from suppliers, fill these in on the Budget Planner (Table 2 on pages 218-224), or on the table you have downloaded from www.gay-friendly-wedding-venues.com/budget.

The remainder of the book focuses on you and the final details of the big day – confirming arrangements with suppliers, choosing outfits, buying wedding rings, and preparing yourself mentally and physically. You will need to decide what happens on the day, who is going to play key roles, and what to say in your speeches. Examples are given of a timetable for the day, a running order and ideas for speeches, as well as helpful lists to ensure nothing gets forgotten.

Finally, in the Directory of Useful Resources you'll find details of books, websites and organisations.

Use this book as a trusted friend throughout your planning process – it will provide useful guidance, vital checklists and key questions to ask venues and suppliers. It will also help you to prepare practically, mentally and physically for one of the most important days of your life. Enjoy the planning – it is all part of the excitement in the build-up to your perfect pink wedding.

Countdown timetable

12 months to go

- Check legal implications of a civil partnership
- Create a wish list
- Celebrate your decision – organise the engagement party
- Set a maximum budget
- Work out a timetable
- Consider using a wedding planner

11 months to go

- Think about themes
- Choose a venue
- Give notice of your Civil Partnership at your local registry office (England, Wales and Northern Ireland only)
- Look at catering options

10 months to go

- Send out 'save the date' cards
- Take out wedding insurance
- Sort out legal and financial administration

9 months to go

- Book your honeymoon

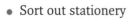

- Sort out stationery
- Look into gift lists

8 months to go

- Sort out catering arrangements
- Book a marquee, if needed

7 months to go

- Book: – Photographers
       – Videographers
       – Website designers

6 months to go

- Book: – Musicians
       – Entertainers
       – Toastmasters
       – Blessing celebrants
- Order your cake
- If having outfits made, visit tailor/dressmaker

5 months to go

- Book: – Transport
       – Decorations
       – Flowers

4 months to go

- Buy/organise: – Outfits
              – Accessories
              – Rings

3 months to go

- Give notice of your Civil Partnership at your local registry office (Scotland only)
- Prepare mentally and physically for the day
- Send out invitations
- Organise readings, speeches and roles
- Prepare detailed plans for the day

2 months to go

- Organise stag dos or hen nights
- Sort out any necessary visas or medication for honeymoon

1 month to go

- Confirm with suppliers
- Confirm arrangements for honeymoon
- Meet registrar
- Book beauty treatments
- Liaise with attendants
- Practice speeches, dances, etc.
- Sort out household arrangements while away

The Civil Partnership Act 2004

This chapter outlines what the act means in terms of rights and responsibilities. You will find it useful if you want to check out legal facts. It also covers your rights if you want to get married abroad.

What the act means – your rights and responsibilities

The Civil Partnership Act 2004 allows same-sex couples, aged 16 and over, who form a civil partnership the same rights as married couples in the following areas:

- Tax, including inheritance tax
- Employment benefits
- Bereavement benefits. When one person dies, their civil partner will be eligible to receive survivor pensions in public service schemes and contracted-out pension schemes from 1988
- Most state and occupational pension benefits
- Income-related benefits, tax credits and child support
- Duty to provide reasonable maintenance for any children of the family
- Ability to apply for parental responsibility for your civil partner's child
- Inheritance of a tenancy agreement, i.e. tenancy succession rights

- Recognition under intestacy rules
- Access to fatal accidents compensation
- Protection from domestic violence
- Recognition in the UK for immigration and nationality purposes
- Exemption from testifying against each other in a court of law
- Next-of-kin visiting rights in hospitals

For further information see the Directory of Useful Resources, pages 203–205.

Frequently asked questions

You will find answers to frequently asked questions below, but if you have any doubts, you should consult a solicitor or financial adviser, or – if you can cope with the legal jargon – the Act itself at: www.opsi.gov.uk.

Q: How does a civil partnership differ from a heterosexual marriage?

A: A civil partnership can only be formed between two people of the same sex.

A civil partnership is formed when each partner has signed the civil partnership document in the presence of a registrar and two witnesses. A marriage is formed when partners exchange spoken vows and also sign the register.

Same-sex couples cannot have a religious service during the registration and it cannot take place in any religious premises. They can, however, have a blessing after the ceremony, although this cannot be held at a registry office.

A same-sex couple who want to marry abroad and have their status as civil partners recognised in the UK, can only do so in countries specified in Schedule 20 of the Civil Partnership Act (see pages 31–33).

If a civil partnership ends, the couple can seek a dissolution rather than a divorce.

Adultery is not allowed as a ground for dissolution, mainly because there is no legal definition of gay sex.

Non-consummation is not a ground for dissolution.

Q: Are civil partnerships available throughout the UK?
A: The Civil Partnership Act applies to England, Wales, Scotland and Northern Ireland.

Q: Who can register?
A: Same-sex couples who are both aged 16 or over and are not already in a civil partnership or marriage. You cannot form a civil partnership if you are related to each other in any of the following ways: adoptive child, adoptive parent, child, former adoptive child, former adoptive parent, grandparent, grandchild, parent, parent's sibling, sibling, sibling's child. Sibling means a brother, sister, half-brother or half-sister. If you have changed gender and have a full Gender Recognition Certificate, you can have a civil partnership.

Q: Do I need permission if I'm under 18?
A: In England, Wales and Northern Ireland, people aged 16 and 17 have to obtain the written consent of their parent(s) or legal guardian(s) before registering a civil partnership. In Scotland, individuals aged 16 or over can register their partnership without the need for parental consent.

Q: What will it cost?
A: You have to pay a set fee to give notice of your civil partnership (currently £30 per person), and there is also a minimum fee to

register the civil partnership (£40 per couple) and to receive a copy of the certificate (£3.50). There is a statutory fee (currently £43.50) if you just want to sign the schedule in front of the registrar in their office. However, if you want a ceremony in a council room, most council offices have a choice of rooms that you can hire, from a committee room to the council chambers. You will pay different rates depending on the council and the size of the room, but the fee will include the hire of the room and the registrar's time.

If you want the registrar to attend an approved wedding venue, you will have to pay a fee for their time, which is set by the individual local authority. This may vary, depending on the day of the week and how far they have to travel. Sometimes they charge more for weekends.

Q: Do we need to be living together in order to register our partnership?
A: No.

Q: What will we be called after we register our partnership?
A: Legally you will be 'civil partners'.

Q: How will I refer to my partner's relatives after the civil partnership ceremony?
A: They are legally referred to as your mother-in-law, brother-in-law, etc.

Q: What if we own two properties in the UK?
A: Only one property owned by a couple, whether that property is owned solely or jointly, may be treated as the principal private residence of either of them at any time for Capital Gains Tax purposes and thus qualify for private residence relief.

Q: Will my civil partnership be publicised?

A: When you give notice of your intention to register a civil partnership, details from the notice will be available in a registry office for public inspection (as for straight marriage), but the details will not include the address of you or your partner (see Book the registrar, page 91).

Q: Can my partner and I form a civil partnership in the UK even if we've already formed an overseas relationship that would be recognised in the UK?

A: It will not be necessary to form a civil partnership in the UK if your existing overseas relationship is treated as a civil partnership.

Q: Do my partner and I need to register as civil partners even if one of us isn't a UK or EEA (European Economic Area) citizen?

A: If you are not an EEA national and require permission to enter or remain in the UK, you will be subject to the same immigration control as straight couples.

- To give notice of a civil partnership with a non-EEA citizen, you will be required to meet one of the following criteria:
- Have entry clearance granted expressly for the purpose of registering a civil partnership in the UK. This is granted by the British Embassy or High Commission in your own country. It will usually be shown as a visa or travel document in your passport; or
- Have the written permission of the Home Secretary to register a civil partnership in the UK. This will usually be issued if you have been granted leave to enter or remain in the UK for over six months; or

- Fall within a class of persons specified by the Home Secretary – for example, you have settled status in the UK, or you were formally spouses but your marriage has been annulled because one of you has changed gender.

These restrictions do not apply if you are a foreigner who has been given the right of abode in the UK, or who is exempt from immigration controls because of your employment.

Registrars are required to report any civil partnership to the Immigration Service if they have suspicions that it is being entered into as a means of circumventing immigration control.

For further information, visit the Immigration and Nationality Directorate, part of the Home Office website at www.ind.homeoffice.gov.uk, or consult an immigration lawyer.

For more information about visa applications, visit the UK Visas website at: www.ukvisas.gov.uk

Q: What happens if my partner dies?
A: If one of you dies after you have registered your partnership, the surviving partner will automatically be recognised under inheritance tax rules. You will have the right to register the death of your partner and will be eligible for bereavement benefits. You will also have the right to claim a survivor pension. You will have tenancy succession rights and will be able to claim compensation for fatal accidents or criminal injuries.

Q: What about my existing Will?
A: Civil partner registration will render an existing Will invalid unless it has been written allowing for the intention to form a civil partnership. If you are planning to register your partnership, arrange for new Wills to be made as a priority.

Q: Can we have a civil partnership without giving notice?

A: Only on medical grounds if one of you is terminally ill and not expected to survive the normal notice period.

Q: Can I change my name?

A: One of you can change your surname to take your partner's. You should be able to use your civil partnership certificate as proof – government departments will certainly accept this. If you want to change your name to form a double-barrelled version of both your surnames, you will have to do this by deed poll. For further information, visit www.ukdps.co.uk/. (See also Name change, page 97.)

Q: Can we choose where we have our civil partnership ceremony?

A: You have to conduct a civil partnership in a registry office or at a venue with a civil wedding licence – see exceptions below. (See pages 60 and 92 for information about registry offices and choosing a venue.)

Q: What if one of us is house-bound?

A: You can only have a civil partnership ceremony in your home if you have provided sufficient medical evidence of your disability or illness.

Q: What if one of us is detained in prison or a mental hospital?

A: Special arrangements can be made to hold a civil partnership ceremony in a prison or mental hospital, but you need to present a supporting statement from the management of the prison or mental hospital.

Pre-nuptial agreements

A pre-nuptial or pre-partnership agreement doesn't have any legal standing, but may be considered by a court if you find yourself in the unhappy position of dissolving the partnership. Often people want to draw up pre-nuptials to protect substantial assets.

If a civil partnership breaks up within a few years, a pre-nup might be taken into consideration by a court. However, if you are applying for a dissolution after some years, when circumstances may have changed, a court is unlikely to take much notice of it.

Instead of seeing it as an agreement in case you split up, use it as a way of agreeing on what you want from a relationship. It could be as simple as a list of expectations that you both agree on, including attitudes to money, children, monogamy, visiting relations, property, ill-health, or anything else you can anticipate happening in your relationship – even how often you cook or who books holidays – but don't expect to stick to it rigidly, or that in itself could be a cause for dissolution.

If you decide to draw up a pre-partnership agreement, it is a good idea to involve a family lawyer. Jacqueline D'Hazzard of Engleharts Solicitors says: 'Although pre-partnership agreements are not legally binding, they have the potential to make it clearer and cheaper when dissolving a civil partnership. If a couple breaks up, an agreement may well help keep it out of litigation and make the whole thing less acrimonious. But if the dissolution goes to court, it gives the judge a clear indication of the couple's intentions at the outset, although of course it does depend on the judge how much they take this into account.'

For more information on civil partnerships see General Register Office in the Directory of Useful Resources, page 204.

Marrying abroad

If you fancy the romance of marrying in a foreign city, on a beach, or with a backdrop of mountains, why not opt for a wedding abroad? This will probably mean you have fewer guests, which may make it less expensive, depending on your travel costs, and you can hand over the organising to specialist companies that arrange weddings abroad. The weather may also be more reliable and you can combine it with your honeymoon. Unfortunately, unlike our hettie friends, you can't just pack your bags and pick a destination.

If you decide to marry abroad and you want your relationship to be recognised as a civil partnership in the UK, you need to check if the country where you want to marry is listed in schedule 20 of the Civil Partnership Act, since these are the countries the UK recognises. The schedule should be automatically updated as and when various countries change their laws on same-sex unions; however, this is not always done immediately so you should double-check. The best place to stay up to date with which countries have some form of civil union for same-sex relationships is http:// en.wikipedia.org/ wiki/Same-sex_marriage.

Countries where some form of gay civil union can take place are: Andorra, Argentina, Belgium, certain parts of Brazil, Canada, Colombia, Czech Republic, Denmark, Finland, France, Germany, Iceland, Israel, Luxembourg, Mexico, Netherlands, New Zealand, Norway, Portugal, Slovenia, South Africa, Spain, Sweden, Switzerland, Tasmania, and certain US States.

In the US, New Jersey, Vermont and Connecticut offer civil unions, and California offers domestic partnerships with benefits similar to civil unions. Massachusetts is the only state to allow same-sex marriages. Even in countries where you are allowed a same-sex marriage, such as Canada, it will be considered only as a civil partnership in the UK. Bear in mind that there may be restrictions within each country about residency requirements. Vermont, Canada and New Zealand are the easiest places to organise the legal ceremonies, as the paperwork can all be done in advance. Vermont is particularly easy since there is no residency period requirement after you arrive in the state, making it ideal for couples who want to elope.

In Canada, it is best to opt for the provinces that offer a 'marriage' as opposed to those which have a 'union civile' – these come under French law and have a residency period requirement of around 30 days.

Danny Waine, of travel agent Perfect Gay Honeymoons, says it is much more difficult in European countries other than the UK. 'Although the UK will recognise the overseas relationship on return, the laws of other European countries require one of the partners to be a resident of that particular country. Spain is slightly different – if you own a property there, you can marry anywhere in the country.'

You also need to check out what kind of celebration you are allowed in each country. In Slovenia, for example, the authorities don't allow any guests or ceremony – you just sign a document. The first two gay men to enter into a civil partnership in Slovenia, Mitja Blazic and Niki Kern, called the ceremony 'humiliating', saying it was more like a car registration than a wedding ceremony.

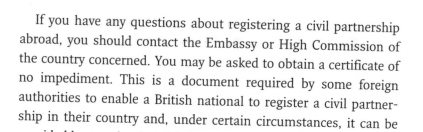

If you have any questions about registering a civil partnership abroad, you should contact the Embassy or High Commission of the country concerned. You may be asked to obtain a certificate of no impediment. This is a document required by some foreign authorities to enable a British national to register a civil partnership in their country and, under certain circumstances, it can be provided by your local registry office.

Once you have tied the knot abroad, you can apply to have your overseas civil partnership documents – with translations, if necessary – sent from the country where it took place and deposited with the General Register Office in the UK. This is a good idea, in case you ever need a copy.

Two conditions apply:

- Your civil partnership has to have taken place in one of the countries listed in Schedule 20.
- One of you must be a British citizen – and only that person can apply to deposit the details.

For further information, contact the Foreign and Commonwealth Office, www.fco.gov.uk (see the Directory of Useful Resources, page 203, for full postal address).

Special circumstances

Members of the Armed Forces can register civil partnerships overseas where a Service Registering Officer is able to offer this service. Currently, this is possible in Australia, Canada, the Falkland Islands, Germany, Gibraltar, Nepal, the US and the Sovereign Base Areas of Akrotiri and Dhekelia.

For more information visit: www.opsi.gov.uk/SI/si2005/20053188.htm

Philip and Michael marrying abroad

When I was younger, I thought one of the good things about being gay was the lack of commitment. As the first countries legalised gay marriage or partnerships, the idea didn't really appeal. But I grew up, and the idea of making a lasting commitment to my partner became as important to me as the equal recognition civil partnerships give to gay couples. Getting married was a great way of dealing with the non-romantic practical issues. In an instant, it gave us equal joint ownership of the flat I owned, avoided inheritance tax if I died, and next-of-kin visiting rights should one of us end up in hospital. And, of course, it was also a big romantic gesture!

We decided to get married in Canada because, although we live in London, my partner comes from Canada. So for our London friends and family it would be a fun trip to Toronto, and for our Canadian friends and Michael's family, it kind of made up for not seeing them as much. Also, it was in the summer of 2005, before it was legal in the UK – a small but important technical point. But we did it knowing that our Canadian gay marriage would be recognised (as a civil partnership) in the UK, which was important, too. If it was just a token thing, I don't think we would have done it.

Getting married abroad also had the unforeseen advantage that because we were planning an event on the other side of the Atlantic, we couldn't get too involved in the organisation. We found the venue, the caterer and the officiant on the Internet. When we spoke to René, our caterer, on the phone, we realised pretty quickly that we could trust her, and that she understood what we wanted. So we were able to delegate some pretty major decisions to her: the colour scheme at the venue and flower arrangements, for example.

And as a present for our guests, we found a cake company in Toronto that made 'gingerbread couples' – usually a man and wife – in gingerbread, iced to match what the bride and groom were wearing. We asked for a same-sex gingerbread couple and, without batting an eyelid, they made 80 of them for us, each iced by hand with the same suits, ties, shirts and shoes as we wore on the day. Our guests loved them.

On the day, I was nervous and it all went far too quickly, but I remembered my boss telling me beforehand that it would be the one day in my life when you're in a room filled with people who love you, and who you love. He was right, and it was a great feeling. I remember at one point watching my mum dancing in a line of our gay friends to 'It's Raining Men' and thinking to myself: perhaps this is it, the moment I dreamt of as a teenager, but that I barely imagined would ever happen – total acceptance of my life in all its parts by everyone in it. As a celebration, and in hope for the future, it was unrivalled.

Philip Reay-Smith, TV news reporter

Registration of civil partnership by Civil Partnership Officer (a British consular officer)

You can register a civil partnership in any country or territory outside the UK in the presence of a Civil Partnership Officer, if the following conditions are met:

- At least one of the proposed civil partners is a United Kingdom national.
- The proposed civil partners would have been eligible to register as civil partners of each other in the relevant part of the United Kingdom.
- The authorities of the country or territory in which it is proposed that they register as civil partners will not object to the registration.
- Insufficient facilities exist for them to enter into an overseas relationship under the law of that country or territory.

For more information visit: www.opsi.gov.uk/si/si2005/20052761. htm.

Top tips

- Remember to take out travel and wedding insurance as soon as you make the booking (see Legal and financial considerations, pages 96–98).
- Combine your ceremony with the honeymoon to cut down on travel costs.
- Check out legal implications and residency requirements.
- Make a group booking on travel and accommodation to reduce costs.

First steps

This chapter is about celebrating your decision and starting to dream about your wedding day. The first steps are great fun: creating a wish list for your perfect day – decide if you want a fairy tale castle, an intimate celebration, hundreds of friends and spectacular fireworks – it's your big chance to fulfil your fantasy.

Celebrate your decision

If you are building up the courage to pop the question, you can either plan a complete surprise in a romantic location, or have a general discussion with your partner about civil partnerships, so that you come to a mutual agreement. I think the change in the law has presented quite a challenge to couples to decide how committed they are to each other. Either way, once you've made it, you will want to celebrate your decision. Then there's the proposal, choosing an engagement ring, announcing your decision to friends and family and throwing a party – a lot of exciting things to think about.

Now is also a good time to have a really frank conversation about what you both want from your lives. To help structure your ideas, write down all the things you both want to be, have and do in the next five, ten, fifteen and twenty years. See how your lists compare and see where you might need to compromise.

Whatever your strategy, at some point, you need to take the plunge. There is a lot of etiquette involved in traditional engagements, such as one of you getting down on one knee, telling parents first, and not wearing your ring until the engagement is announced publicly. As with any of the straight wedding traditions, you can decide what bits you want to pick out, or you can completely re-write the rule book – most of it can't apply easily because it is so gender-specific, but there are ways to adapt it.

If you are popping the question, you may wish to choose a significant date or time – for example, when you are on holiday, on New Year's Eve, or the anniversary of when you met. Make it special and memorable.

James and John

James and John, were on a six-week round-the-world trip of a lifetime, when James decided to pop the question on their last night. 'I had bought a platinum ring before we left, but it was a bit stressful, making sure John didn't find it in the luggage or it wasn't stolen.' James set the whole scene up beautifully, as the couple were staying in a private villa within an exclusive hotel complex in Bali. He ordered champagne, set up his I-pod with speakers to play music from the film they first saw together, *Beautiful Thing*, and asked John to be his lifetime partner. John says: 'I was so overwhelmed; James took me totally by surprise.' He added: 'I had been a bit sceptical about civil partnerships at first, thinking it was too conformist, but after he asked me, I felt so excited and couldn't wait for our big day.'

(See also page 65 for details of their ceremony.)

Engagement rings

According to tradition, an engagement ring is supposed to cost the equivalent of one month's salary. Depending on how much you earn, this could be a very expensive purchase. Whatever your income, can you afford to spend a whole month's salary on top of planning for the wedding? Some would argue that it is better to spend money on the ring rather than the wedding, since the former will last a lifetime and the latter just one day.

If you do want to surprise your loved one with an engagement ring, you can find out their finger size using a handy online chart at www.yellobox.co.uk/ringchart.asp. To find an approximate ring size, take a ring your partner already owns and place it over the circles on the chart until you find one that is closest. The circles represent the size of the internal diameter of the ring. If you are off for a shopping trip to Paris or New York, you will need an international converter. Luckily there is another handy chart: www.yellobox.co.uk/ringsizes.asp

If you don't feel confident about this method and can 'borrow' one of your partner's rings, take it to a jewellers and ask them to measure it. Or try one of your partner's rings on and see where it comes to on your finger, then mark this with a pen.

Whatever you do, make sure the ring can be adjusted later if you haven't got the size quite right. It also depends which finger they want to wear it on. In the hetty world, you wear an engagement ring on the finger next to the little finger, on your left hand. Some gay couples choose to use that finger, or the same one on the right hand, or a different finger altogether. It's up to you and depends if you want to tell the world you are married by following convention, or retain some privacy, or just be different.

Diamonds are a girl's best friend Traditionally, engagement rings involve diamonds. 'There are four features that determine the worth of a diamond – the carat, clarity, cut and colour. The most important of these are colour and clarity,' says Malcolm Cooper of Ampalian Jewellers.

Carat refers to the weight of a diamond. It is important that this is not confused with karat, the term used to describe the purity of gold – 24-karat gold is pure gold. Clarity refers to the number of imperfections and their visibility to the naked eye, while the cut is used to describe the shape or outline of a diamond's front. Seventy-five per cent of all diamond gemstones today have the shape known as Round Brilliant – the most common shape for engagement rings.

Entirely colourless diamonds are supremely rare and precious – most diamonds have some trace of body colour, and many are quite deeply coloured.

Another 'C' to ask about is conflict. The campaign group Amnesty says: 'Conflict diamonds are those sold in order to fund armed conflict and civil war.'

The charity has produced a guide explaining how consumers can make a difference. It recommends that shoppers ask retailers the following questions about the diamonds they are buying:

- Do you know where the diamonds you sell come from?
- Can I see a copy of your company's policy on conflict diamonds?
- Can you show me a written guarantee from your diamond suppliers that shows that your diamonds are conflict-free?
- How can I be sure that none of your jewellery contains conflict diamonds?

You can access the guide on www.amnesty.org.uk.

You may want to choose a ring with a gem related to each other's star sign. There is a handy table at www.yellowbox.co.uk/superstitious.asp

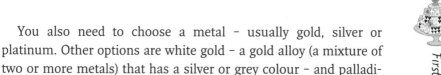

You also need to choose a metal – usually gold, silver or platinum. Other options are white gold – a gold alloy (a mixture of two or more metals) that has a silver or grey colour – and palladium (platinum metal group alloyed with gold), which some jewellers are using to make rings and which is cheaper than gold or platinum.

If you both want a ring, expect to spend a Saturday shopping. In London, the main street for jewellery is Hatton Garden, a street in Clerkenwell. There are nearly 300 jewellery businesses in the area with the UK's highest density of diamond shops (see www. hatton-garden.net). In addition to high street stores, there are plenty of online jewellers, or you can design and make your own rings at www.weddingringworkshop.co.uk.

Think about your personal circumstances and preferences, but don't see the buying of rings as a test of how much you love each other.

When you get your estimates keep them in a file or record them in the Budget Planner (Table 2 on page 223), and then when you have decided on the best price and supplier, fill in the final column of the Budget Planner. You can also download the table from www.gay-friendly-wedding-venues.com/budget.

Start spreading the news

Decide who you wish to tell first about your good news. If you aren't sure of how some of your relatives will react, think about telling close friends before family. Some people send out engagement cards. You can find some gay-themed ones on www.lavenderlifestyles.co.uk. Or you can put an announcement in the 'hatches, matches and dispatches' sections of the press – either in your local paper, in a national newspaper, or in the pink press. Newspapers generally want the written consent of both parties before publishing an engagement notice. The traditional place for announcements is *The Times* newspaper. They are usually charged on a per word basis, with a minimum word count of 10 words, while photos or boxes around the text are charged extra.

Make sure you are happy to be outed locally, as you may attract some media attention. The local papers may want to feature your wedding, especially if it's near the anniversary of the law changing.

When you get your estimates, fill them in on Table 2 Budget Planner, page 218, and then when you have decided which paper to put your announcement in, fill in the final column on the plan or on the table you have downloaded.

A cheaper option is to get on the phone and tell family and friends, or send out an e-mail, or a 'save the date' card (see page 102).

Think through how you are going to tell anyone who doesn't know you well, or those who might have a less positive response. Do you want to meet face-to-face to get an immediate reaction that you can respond to and thrash out, or do you prefer a letter or e-mail to give people time to digest the news? In some circumstances, it might be a bit like coming out again, or it may actually be coming out for the first time to some members of your family or colleagues. It is an emotional time, but try not to let anyone spoil the enjoyment of planning your wedding.

Throwing an engagement party

Getting hitched is a great excuse for a party and it can be a good trial run to see who behaves badly! You can make it quite informal at your local gay bar, or at home, or have a lavish event in the private function room of a restaurant or hotel. You'll find gay-friendly venues at www.gay-friendly-wedding-venues.com.

Think about who you are inviting to the engagement party – will they expect an invitation to the wedding? If you can't invite every-

Seraphina

We don't normally like being the centre of attention, but it was really nice having people from different parts of our life meeting each other for the first time, getting on really well and 'celebrating' us.

We've been pretty lucky with our parents. My father has always been alright about it, though I'm sure he's privately disappointed, and my partner's parents have been great after a very shaky start. We were very surprised when my father described the day as 'a sort of wedding' and my partner's parents were miffed that they weren't included in the actual ceremony! That's been very touching and it was just very nice to realise that everyone was so pleased for us.

I guess my advice would be – if you know you want to be together, DO IT! And make sure that the day is for you and you do it your way. Savour it and try to remember as much of it as possible.

Somehow I feel even more entwined with my partner (dare I say 'wedded'!) but can't really say why, it just feels different in a very nice way. Perhaps it's about validation and knowing that you are legally recognised. I like the fact that my partner is now my legal next-of-kin. And I still think of her as my partner – we don't do the 'wife' thing!

Seraphina Granelli, Retailer, London

one, you might need to make it clear that the wedding will be for family and close friends only. If you do want to invite everyone, you may need to do some homework first to work out your budget, etc. (See Decide who to invite, page 52.)

When you get your estimates fill them in on Table 2 Budget Planner, page 218, and then when you have decided on the venue for your party, fill in the final column of the planner. (Or use the table you have downloaded).

Create a wish list

Before you start to look for venues, or decide who to invite, each of you should draw up a wish list of the kind of wedding you would like, and then see how your lists compare. Use Table 1 Wedding Wish List on pages 216–217 to each create your ideal day.

Set a maximum budget

Once you've settled on a potential number of guests, get the calculator out. It might make you change your mind and invite two witnesses and have a swift half down the pub. As an example, if you just think in terms of catering at £35 a head and drink at £15, 80 guests would cost £4,000 before you've hired a venue, bought a suit or frock, or been driven off in a Roller en route to your safari honeymoon. Of course, this may sound cheap to some. Elton John and his partner were reported to have spent £55,000 on their rings alone. Straight weddings are said to cost on average around £18,000. At the other extreme, the minimum cost is the amount needed for the civil partnership licence and to register the partnership – around £100–£150.

To get your head around how much you are going to spend, turn to the Budget Planner, Table 2, in the resources section on pages 218–224 and allocate a rough idea of how much you want to spend on the options you are considering for your wedding – for example, maximum on catering £5,000. Think through the day to work out everything you want and how much you are willing to spend on it.

Once you have allocated an amount to each of the items, you then need to obtain quotations from suppliers. Fill in the third column of the Budget Planner with your names if want to divide up the task of finding quotations. Prices will vary enormously depending on location, style of wedding, time of year and day of the week. For example, you can often halve the price of a venue by holding your ceremony on Monday through to Thursday. See more money-saving tips on pages 46–48.

Before you plunge into getting price quotations, read the relevant sections of the book to find out what questions to ask the suppliers, how to save money, and, if you want to really splash out on your big gay day, ideas for extravagant options. When you start to get your estimates keep a file or use the Budget Planner to record them. Complete the final column in the Budget Planner (table 2 on pages 218–224) when you have decided which suppliers and items to buy. (This plan is also available as an electronic spreadsheet on www.gay-friendly-wedding-venues.com/budget.)

Next, think about starting a new wedding bank account. This will make it easier to manage the financing of your big day. You can pay into it regularly, write one cheque to each supplier and hopefully avoid arguing about money.

Most gay and lesbian couples will probably be paying for their own wedding, but if anyone else is contributing financially, I'd recommend allocating specific items to them to spend their money on, such as the flowers or the transport. This will hopefully reduce the risk of them dictating the detail of your day. I've seen at first hand, from my experience of working in a hotel, the stress of parents taking over the show because they are paying.

Once you start spending, keep a close eye on your budget and if you overspend in one area, find somewhere else on the budget to claw this money back.

Keeping costs down

Any celebration involving hiring a venue, supplying food and drink, etc., can become very expensive, so here are some money-saving tips:

Timing
- Hold the ceremony on a weekday, or out of the peak season. Some consider this to be April to October, although the peak months are June, July and August, and December can be very busy at some venues because of Christmas events.
- If you want to go for the less popular months of January, February, March and November, good rates can be negotiated at venues, especially if the wedding is booked at the last minute.
- Book before January, when prices often increase.

Don't mention weddings
- For some items, such as transport or even cakes, don't mention the word 'wedding' if you can avoid it when asking for quotations – otherwise the price will inevitably go up.

Friends
- Go through the list of items on the Budget Planner and see if you can ask friends to do any of the jobs. However, make sure you are confident they can carry out the job. There is always a risk that they aren't as good as they say, or are sick on the day, or, worse still, that you fall out with them.

Negotiate discounts

- Go to wedding fairs – suppliers will often offer a discount if booked on the day.
- If a number of guests are staying at the venue where you are holding the reception, negotiate a discount on bedrooms.
- Always ask if venues and suppliers can offer you a better price.

Cut out extras

- Cut out the peripheries such as favours, or disposable cameras, as they often get wasted.
- Serve sparkling wine rather than champagne.

Sharing costs

- If you are having a wedding in a venue that has several celebrations over the same time period, consider sharing the costs of flowers and decorations.
- Another option is to have a joint wedding. If you have very close friends who are also planning a civil partnership, it is worth considering as long as you can all agree on the format. This way you share the cost of all the suppliers and halve the workload.

Go 'vintage' or second-hand

- If you don't mind second-hand wedding items, there are loads of bargains to be had. I typed in 'wedding' on www.ebay.co.uk and 29,466 items came up. Even when I searched for something as specific as wedding chair covers, 31 items came up.
- Borrow from people who have recently had weddings or big events.

Have a cheap honeymoon

- Go away for a romantic weekend and save the once-in-a-lifetime trip for when you have more money.
- Do a house swap with friends.
- Go camping.

Consider being featured in the media
- If you're not shy, you could offer to be a case study in a TV show or magazine – you may get a free makeover, props or photography.

Keep the numbers down
- If money is tight, be strict about who you invite and make sure you keep control of the price per head. Have a story that you both stick to, such as only family and friends have been invited and no colleagues. You could always hold a separate party at home for work friends or wider circles, where people bring a bottle or a dish to contribute to a buffet.

Hire don't buy
- Hiring wedding outfits, in particular, is much cheaper than buying. You can also hire decorations, plants, etc.

If you do buy, wait for the sales
- Go shopping after Christmas for decorations, especially fairy lights, or wait for the summer sales for outfits.
- Look out for designer clothes sales or visit factory shops.

Check prices
- Always check if prices include VAT and service. Smaller companies won't charge VAT. Remember this adds $17\frac{1}{2}$ per cent to your bill. Make sure when you compare prices that you are looking at like-for-like products or services.

Work out a timetable

After you've recovered from getting down on one knee and popping the question and the champagne corks, you need to start planning a timetable to prepare for the big day. There is a lot more to it than you realise, but if you make a month-by-month or even week-by-

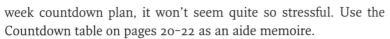
week countdown plan, it won't seem quite so stressful. Use the Countdown table on pages 20-22 as an aide memoire.

You can pick and choose the elements you want to incorporate into your wedding plan, but the key thing is to have a wedding organising system or tool, which could be a spreadsheet, diary or

Clare says, make it unique

Apart from making a statement to each other and to the rest of the world about your devotion and commitment, civil partnership is your chance to share your happiness with everyone you love. You do not *have* to follow any set pattern, invite extended family, wear a big white dress, or have a cake – you can if you wish, but you can use your imagination to create a celebration that is truly unique.

You can make your civil partnership exactly what you want to make it, which is incredibly liberating, and you do not have to apologise for anything, feel any sense of shame or embarrassment – feelings with which so many gay couples battle as they find their relationships compared unfavourably with straight couples.

To be able to make this promise in public and in law is the biggest step towards equality that gay couples have ever known, but it brings with it responsibility as well as freedom. You are promising to maintain the love and respect you have for one another through good as well as bad times. That promise matters, and although not every couple will stay together forever, by undertaking civil partnership they are making a strong statement of intent.

Clare Balding, TV sports presenter

wall planner, marking out essential activities with deadlines and who is responsible for achieving them. You also need a filing system for the paperwork you will accumulate once you start to gather estimates, brochures and contracts from venues and suppliers.

Allocate specific days or evenings in the week when you are going to work on your wedding plan, but also remember to have time out.

However much time you allow, always build in a contingency in case, for example, caterers don't come back quickly with quotations, you can't find the service you require, or there is some outside force such as a postal strike, snow, or family crisis. The best-laid plans always need to allow for unforeseen circumstances.

Jamie and Mike's theatrical performance

Jamie and Mike gave themselves only five months to organise the whole show – it took every spare moment, but they loved the build-up. They looked at three theatres that have civil wedding licences and decided on the London Palladium. 'You can't actually get married on stage, but it has a Cinderella Room, which seemed appropriate. It was gold and shiny, so camp – perfect for us,' says Jamie.

Mike wrote a script for the whole day, including what the registrar would say. They both researched a wide range of poems, quotations and song lyrics and put together a programme, which was presented like a performance with references to cast and crew, the First and Second Acts. They had two meetings with the registrar before the event and he was very enthusiastic, as it was his first civil partnership. 'He was superb,' says Jamie. They also met with all the senior staff at the theatre.

The First Act – the ceremony – was held in the Variety Room, and as they entered the room, Jamie's sister sang 'Over the Rainbow'. Two of their closest friends played the roles of flower girl and ring boy, their friends gave short speeches about what their friendship with the pair meant to them, and Jamie and Mike then said a dedication to each other, using theatrical allusions.

This was followed by a cocktail party in the Cinderella Room, with canapés provided by the theatre and, as the speeches ended, a group from the London Gay Men's Chorus provided the music. At 5.30pm they had to leave the theatre because it had a performance that night, so friends and family helped to clear up the props and shove them in a taxi back to Jamie's brother's hotel, while half the guests joined Jamie and Mike in a procession up to Old Compton Street, the heart of gay Soho, to have a drink at their favourite bar.

After the drink, 30 close family members went to The Ivy restaurant for a champagne reception followed by dinner. At 11.30pm, the party ended and they piled into cabs to get home. Jamie's sister, mother and father had decorated Jamie and Mike's bedroom in red material with rose petals and glitter on the bed and had lit candles around the room and placed a bottle of champagne by the bedside. A perfect end to a perfect day.

(You can see photos, copies of the invitation and programme on their website, www.mikeandjamie.co.uk)

Setting the date

If you want to hold your wedding on a popular date in the summer, you may need to plan at least a year in advance. For example, 07-07-07 was a particularly popular date, but any Saturday from June to September can be booked up even two years ahead of time. (See also Book the registrar, page 91.)

Refer to the Countdown timetable on pages 2--22 to give you an idea of what to book and in what order, and to see if your proposed timetable is feasible. You will probably need to revise this as you go along, but by putting everything in your diary, nothing will be missed off the list.

Laura and I booked our venue and the registry office a year in advance, but did most of the organising in the last six months. Jamie and Mike, a gay couple based in London organised a huge theatrical wedding in under five months – see pages 50–51.

Decide who to invite

Refer to your wish list on pages 216–217; if you want an intimate wedding, you may be looking at between 10 and 40 guests, or for an extravaganza, anything up to around 500.

When compiling your list, think of family, friends, work colleagues and other areas of your life, such as sports teams, knitting circles, book clubs, neighbours, drinking mates, ex-lovers, etc. It can soon tot up. You also need to decide if you want to invite partners of colleagues, for example, whom you may not know very well. The other big decision is whether or not to invite children. Our caterers charged full price for children over the age of eight – so they don't come cheap.

After you have compiled your initial list, question who you really want to invite. A friend told me of a good test – if you

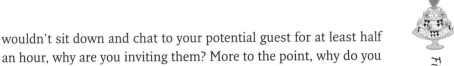

wouldn't sit down and chat to your potential guest for at least half an hour, why are you inviting them? More to the point, why do you want to inflict them on your other guests? (Be careful not to leave the list lying around in case someone pops over and sees they are not on the list, or they have a question mark by their name.)

You may have to limit numbers due to restrictions at the venue. Even if a licensed wedding venue can cater for larger numbers, their wedding licence will specify the maximum number for the ceremony, which is often smaller, so you may want to find the venue first and then decide who to invite.

If you want to invite more people than you can fit in the ceremony room, consider having two or even three sets of invitations, inviting people to the ceremony, the reception and/or the party afterwards. Since it can often be tricky to invite only a few people from your workplace, this might be a way of accommodating more colleagues. If you choose this option, make sure you handle it sensitively so that people don't feel like B-list friends, or arrive in the middle of speeches and feel like a spare part. Try to have a gap between the meal and the evening party, which will also enable you to have a chance to change and have a quick rest.

You may also need to account for a few people who'll invite themselves. People are either overexcited about the thought of attending their first gay wedding, thick-skinned, or desperate for a night out. Either have a ready answer or an elastic budget! You can also rely on at least a certain number of invitees not being able to attend or dropping out.

Make an A-list of people you definitely want to invite and a B-list of people you would like to invite if you can afford to, or if people on your A-list drop out.

Another useful aid is to do a mock table plan. If you find people hard to place, think about whether you really want to invite them.

Consider using a wedding planner

If you are frantically busy with your job, looking after the kids or an elderly relative, or just feel overwhelmed by the thought of planning a gay wedding, you can call in a wedding planner to take the strain. 'Gay wedding planners' is certainly one of the most popular searches that leads to our website, and planners are noticing a marked increase in enquiries from gay couples.

A wedding planner will sit down, preferably with both partners, and work out your specific requirements and budget. You can ask them to take over all the responsibility for planning the wedding, or just specific elements. They will help you with the initial ideas about the style or theme of the day and point you in the right direction to get what you want. If you want them to continue working for you, ask them to do the research and help you select venues and caterers. They can even help with details such as ordering and sending out invitations and managing the replies on a database.

Use the Budget Plan, your wish list and the following checklist as the basis of your discussions and to make sure the planner has thought of everything.

What can a wedding planner do for you?

- Help with initial ideas
- Shortlist venues
- Find suppliers
- Source unusual requests
- Liaise with venues and suppliers
- Coordinate invitations
- Organise the day itself
- Organise the honeymoon

Wedding planner Jenny Barnes, based in Buckinghamshire, says: 'The majority of our clients are either career couples with not much time to spare for organising their wedding, or they are having a wedding at some distance from their home. We carry out the time-consuming tasks, like supplier or venue searches, using our local knowledge. This leaves them free to concentrate on the big decisions and saves them a considerable amount of travelling.'

Usually, wedding planners have good relationships with venues and suppliers, such as florists and entertainers, and can often negotiate a good rate for you. They will gather quotations and liaise with the venue and suppliers throughout the preparation, all the way to the big day. Most wedding planners will attend on the day – from your home to the civil venue to the reception – to make sure everything goes smoothly. If there are any glitches – for example, the drink not being delivered or transport not arriving on time – they should have a string of suppliers they can call on in an emergency. They can even organise the honeymoon for you – which certainly relieves some stress in the middle of planning your wedding, believe me!

If you want something unusual or wacky but don't know where to start, a wedding planner will undertake the research and make sure your dreams can be fulfilled.

They will also be up to date with the latest innovations in the wedding market and can organise the finest level of detail – for example, sourcing ice sculptures, arranging cabaret performers, singing waiters, casino tables or fireworks.

How to budget for a wedding planner

Wedding planners will often provide a range of services, from a two- or three-hour initial discussion of ideas, to a three-month planning service, to full co-ordination, including liaison on the day. Some will charge a set fee for particular services – for example, the initial discussion, finding a venue and each supplier – or offer an overall package for full co-ordination. Others will charge you a fee, but also take commission from the suppliers and venue. Some take a fee based on a set percentage of your spend on the wedding. There are pros and cons with all of these methods, but the last one could work out more expensive if your costs start to escalate. Find out exactly how much they charge and whether they take commission from venues and suppliers.

If you are on a tight budget, you may choose to use a planner for a small element, such as the initial brainstorming meeting. A lot of venues also have wedding co-ordinators who can help with some of the planning and will certainly manage the reception arrangements on the day itself. However, a wedding planner can ensure that the venue provides exactly what you have ordered, will look after the gifts and liaise with the photographer, and do numerous other things that the in-house coordinator might not do.

> **❝ A wedding planner should be able to save you their fee in time or discounts. ❞** Linda Lawcock, of Your Perfect Day, wedding planner

Sometimes another supplier can also act as an unofficial wedding planner for certain aspects of the day. For example, our caterer said he could organise the flowers and decoration as he often worked with companies he knew and could negotiate a discount for us. He also organised all the napkins and tablecloths to co-ordinate with the colour scheme.

Alternatively, on the day itself you can hire a toastmaster (see page 141), who is trained to ensure that events run smoothly by liaising with all the suppliers and organising your guests. This is what we did and it took away all the worry of hosting the event. Our toastmaster arrived at the reception venue while we were at the registry office. He made sure all the decorations were in place and the caterers were going to be ready on time. He then welcomed the guests, introduced speakers and liaised with the photographer, band and venue manager to make sure everything went like clockwork. However, we spent a lot of time organising the wedding in advance and had fully briefed the toastmaster, so if you are short of time in the run up to your big day, I'd recommend using a wedding planner.

When you get your estimates keep them in a file or record in the Budget Planner (table 2 on pages 218–224), and then when you have decided on the best price and supplier, fill in the final column of the Budget Planner. You can also download the table from www.gay-friendly-wedding-venues.com/budget.

Top tip

- Whatever your budget, agree a set fee and make sure you have a detailed account of the wedding planner's services and responsibilities.

3 Big decisions

Once you have taken the first steps of creating a wish list, deciding how many people to invite and how much to spend, you can venture out into the world to make your wedding a reality – choose the venue, decide on catering and book the registrar. This stage is very exciting as it all begins to feel very real.

Think about themes and styles

The next step, once you've set the budget, is to decide on the theme or style of your wedding. You can really have some fun and let your imagination run wild – it's your big gay day. The theme or style can determine the venue, stationery, how you decorate the room, how you or your guests dress, the food, transport, music – the possibilities are endless. You can base your theme on anything you fancy – from the time of year to your favourite film or a particular passion. It can be something simple like a choice of colour or symbol, through to an elaborate fantasy.

For example, if you are thinking of holding your civil partnership around Christmas time, you could follow the lead of comedy actor Matt Lucas and have a pantomime theme at your civil partnership. He and his partner, Kevin McGee, dressed up as Aladdin and Prince Charming. Over 400 guests came in fancy dress with actress Barbara Windsor as a fairy godmother and singer Will Young as an ugly sister. Sir Elton John and his civil partner, David Furnish, also appeared as Captain Hook and Prince Charming.

Companies that specialise in staging events will dress a room in any style for you, even employing lookalikes of famous people to wander around the room acting the part. A company I know created an underwater theme with a centrepiece of a submarine with water running around it, big helium fish hanging from the ceiling and the backdrop of a coral reef. They used special lighting effects as well as fake fish skins as tablecloths. Another client wanted the theme from the TV show *Only Fools and Horses*, so they had a Reliant Robin as the centrepiece and Rodney and Del Boy look-alikes wandering around. Other wedding themes the company has created include a James Bond set, a fairy's grotto and a Sri Lankan temple.

You can, of course, make or buy your own props. eBay and second-hand or retro shops are good sources of memorabilia. If you want to create a fantasy setting for your wedding, get some inspiration by watching relevant films, going to museums, reading books and magazines, or searching the Internet to see how people dressed in different eras.

Here are some more ideas, from the simple to extravagant. Incorporate the theme into your invitations, menu cards, order of ceremony, place names, table and room decorations, and even your outfits and jewellery.

Gay symbols Weave your theme around one of the recognised gay symbols, such as rainbows, black triangles, pink triangles, two male or female gender symbols joined together, or the labrys – the double-bladed axe symbolising lesbian love.

Gay icons Choose your theme based on gay icons, with the room decoration inspired by their style. Match your outfits to theirs, and play music performed by them or featured in their films.

Here's a list of further ideas:

- Annual events such as Pride festivals
- Colour – rainbows or pink
- Camp theme –think feathers, flamingoes, drag kings and queens
- Country and western – line dancing in a country barn
- Nationality or ethnicity – from Scottish to Indian
- Pagan wedding – do something different
- Weekend house party – for that exclusive feel
- Era – 1920s flapper girls or 60s swingers

For more on gay symbols, visit www.lambda.org/symbols. htm. For more ideas on themes, visit www.gay-friendly-wedding-venues.com/gaywedding.

Find a venue

Once you have an idea of budget and how many people you want to invite, you can start looking for a venue to accommodate your 500 close friends! Your ideas might change once you have looked at a few, so keep an open mind. You may find you fall in love with somewhere that can hold only 50 people, or one that is so expensive you can afford to invite only 20.

You may be looking for a venue to suit either your theme or the timing of your wedding. For example, if you want a winter wedding, you might choose a castle that is dressed for Christmas, or a summer wedding would suit a country house with grounds.

For the actual civil partnership ceremony, you can use any registry office or licensed wedding venue in the country. This means that they hold a civil wedding licence, not an alcohol licence, but obviously both are important. If you don't fancy the municipal nature of some registry offices, they will give you a list of licensed wedding venues in the area – there are over 3,500 of them in the UK, ranging from castles to racecourses, hotels to country barns, and even the London Eye.

You can search for licensed wedding venues by postcode or town on the General Register Office website:

- in England and Wales at: www.gro.gov.uk
- in Scotland at: www.gro-scotland.gov.uk/files1/registration/approved-places-for-civil-marriage-by-council.html
- and in Northern Ireland at: http://www.groni.gov.uk/Publication/1712007102234.pdf

A good site for finding unusual venues listed by category is www.civilvenuesuk.com.

Some licensed venues are promoting themselves as gay-friendly. You can look on www.gay-friendly-wedding venues.com, of course, or other websites, such as www.pinkweddings.biz or www.modern-commitments.co.uk.

All licensed wedding venues have a limit on the number of people who can attend the ceremony, even if they can actually cater for more. So you may want to have the ceremony at a registry office and then the reception at another venue, inviting some people to the ceremony and more to the reception.

Wherever you decide to hold the event, you have to 'give notice' of your intention to have a civil partnership at your *local* registry office. (See Book the registrar, page 91.)

Nikki and Donna split the occasion

We wanted the least amount of hassle and consequently chose the easiest and most enjoyable route – which was to split the event. We had the ceremony in April and the reception a few months later at the Royal Society for the Arts in London.

I'd say choose a venue that your guests would find interesting and that has decent public transport links so that they can drink as much as they like without having to worry about driving home. Meet the operations manager/conference manager prior to the event and go through everything in detail. If they aren't helpful, find another venue. On the day, arrive early and go through everything again, make sure all the technical equipment works and that either you know how to use it, or someone will be on hand to put it right. There are bound to be things that go wrong, but your guests don't know what to expect, so just work your way around it... so long as there's plenty of alcohol, no-one will notice!

We didn't really expect a civil partnership to make any difference to our relationship – we saw it as a way of legally protecting each other during the worst of times. Instead, we both agree that the public declaration of our partnership has added depth to our commitment to each other and brought a sense of calm and peace that we didn't even know was missing.

Nikki, Charity Communications Director, London

Types of venues

If money is no object, you can hire a venue such as a castle, country house or stylish restaurant for exclusive use. Some swish venues allow you to arrive by helicopter or private plane, or float down in a hot-air balloon.

Religious buildings You are not yet allowed to hold a civil partnership ceremony in a religious building – it has to be a secular ceremony. However, there are a number of buildings with a wedding licence that are former churches, or that have a spiritual or religious connection. However, you are not allowed to have any religious content in the readings or vows of a civil partnership, although if you can find a celebrant who is willing to officiate, you can have a blessing after the civil ceremony (see Celebrants, page 143).

Gay venues To keep it all 'in the family', you may want to hold your wedding or reception in a gay pub, club, hotel or restaurant. Many can be hired for private functions and some have wedding licences. Additionally, they may already be themed, which will save you decorating them, and they may have sound systems and resident DJs to make sure your party goes with a swing. If you are new to an area, look out for rainbow flags or stickers in windows, or check out the Internet or magazines for local gay listings.

Hotels The vast majority of licensed wedding venues are hotels with a choice of room for the ceremony and reception. The advantage is that your guests don't need to stagger far for their accommodation and even if you don't want to stay there, you are usually offered a complimentary room in which to change outfits, have a fag break, or escape from Auntie Maud.

Many hotels offer wedding packages with a per head price that includes drinks, food, room hire, accommodation and all the services you would expect. They usually have a wedding co-ordinator who will talk you through all aspects of the day and can arrange a florist, DJ, red carpet, help with seating plans and be the master or mistress of ceremonies on the day.

If you want a truly relaxing wedding, hold your civil partnership in a spa hotel. Treat yourself to a mud wrap, thermal bath, or dip in an ozone pool before you tie the knot. You can't actually hold the ceremony in the spa, but most are located in hotels, so you can have the formalities in the function rooms and then get your kit off for an unusual reception.

A spa is also a good place to hold your hen or stag night if that is your thing – some have specific days or nights for each gender. See Stag dos and hen nights, page 192.

Castles Imagine tying the knot in a romantic castle with fairy tale turrets, a moat and manicured lawns. Many castles have to be hired on an exclusive basis, which can set you back a few bob, but does provide perfect privacy. Some castles are privately owned and can provide a unique insight into how the other half lives – why not pretend to be queens for the day!

Marquees Some venues, such as licensed hotels or castles that have smaller rooms for the ceremony, often offer the option of hiring a marquee for the party afterwards so that you can entertain more friends.

Country houses If you love a sense of history, a country house can add a touch of class to your wedding day, and if you want a venue on an exclusive-use basis, with plenty of privacy, hiring a country house could be a good answer.

Restaurants Some restaurants have wedding licences, so the ceremony can be swiftly followed by a slap-up meal. However, in any

James and John

Their dream was to get married in a castle with friends and family all around them. They chose Thornbury Castle, just outside Bristol, where they live. Close friends and family stayed the night before in the baronial-style hotel with fabulous four-poster beds. As they held the event on a Sunday in early December, there weren't many other guests, so it felt like they had the castle on an exclusive-use basis without having to pay for that privilege – a saving of several thousand pounds.

James and John entered the oak-panelled library to the theme tune from *Dynasty*, played by a string quartet. The registrar then introduced the ceremony by giving some of the history of the castle. The signing of the register was followed swiftly by a champagne reception, which kept guests occupied while formal photographs were taken. The photographer orchestrated a group shot by climbing up into the rafters of the castle to look down on the guests.

A formal sit-down dinner followed, with the traditional top table and 50 guests on round tables. The room was decorated for Christmas anyway, so that gave a great atmosphere with a big tree, candles and fairy lights. A fireworks display in the castle grounds signalled the grand finale. James and John were then swept off in the castle's Bentley for a half-hour spin – a perfect way to end a sumptuous wedding.

(See also page 38.)

restaurant or venue, you aren't allowed to serve food or drink *before* a civil partnership ceremony, in case you are inebriated by the time you sign on the dotted line! Restaurants can also be a good option for a separate reception since you can often hire them exclusively.

Pubs or inns There are over 100 pubs in the UK with civil wedding licences and, of course, you can usually hire a private room upstairs, or take over the whole venue for a reception.

Village halls and community centres Some village halls have wedding licences so you can conduct the whole event there, but the fact they have a licence usually makes them twice as expensive to hire as an unlicensed hall. A good budget option is to have your reception in the local village hall, especially if friends and family can help with the catering and decorating, although getting caterers in will save you having to clear up after your own wedding. You can probably supply your own booze, so that knocks down the price. Some halls also offer a discount if you live locally.

Think about whether you need to hire a bouncer or someone to keep an eye on security, especially if you have presents or guests' belongings on show. Consider having someone to host or manage the event for you – perhaps hire a toastmaster or appoint a guest as a master of ceremonies, because unlike at other venues, you may not have someone in a management role.

A useful website is www.hallshire.com, which lists more than 400 village halls for hire.

Unusual venues

A good site for finding unusual venues listed by category, such as private schools, is www.civilvenuesuk.com.

Sports venues Many sports venues have excellent catering facilities and some are licensed to hold weddings. Venues range from football clubs and racecourses to golf, sailing and rugby clubs.

However, with any sports venue you should ensure that your preferred date doesn't clash with fixtures, which often take place on the weekends, and aren't always known a long time in advance, being dependent on results. But these venues can provide a grand and stylish setting, with exclusive use midweek or outside the sport's season.

Academic institutions If you fancy sipping champagne in the quad and being punted off down the river to your honeymoon, a number of universities have wedding licences, including some Oxford and Cambridge colleges. Over twenty public schools also have civil wedding licences. You may be restricted to having a wedding outside term-time, but with the long holidays, this should not be too much of a problem.

Museums and arts venues Add a little history to your special day by holding your civil partnership ceremony in a museum. Or, if you like a bit of drama, a number of theatres have civil wedding licences.

You can also get married in some cinemas, galleries, concert halls, arts centres, or film studios.

Private clubs If you like that exclusive feel, a number of private clubs are available for hire.

Ships, boats and piers If you fancy a nautical theme or a captain in uniform, how about a wedding aboard a ship or cruising down the Thames on a pleasure boat?

Zoos and safari parks Some zoos and safari parks have wedding licences and offer unusual options.

Planes, trains and . . . Believe it or not, you can actually get married at an airport. Shoreham Airport is a gay-friendly venue with a civil wedding licence. If you have a pilot licence, you can take off on your honeymoon straight away! You can also tie the knot in the Concorde viewing lounge at Manchester Airport.

If you are a real trainspotter, you can tie the knot at over eight different railway centres.

Gardens or parklands Strictly speaking, a civil partnership has to be indoors; however, it is only the signing of the register that is the legal part. Some venues have engineered it so that the ceremony starts on the terrace overlooking the gardens, with a welcome or reading, and then the couple go inside for the formalities, although guests can still hear the proceedings outside. They then go back out to exchange rings in front of the guests. In the UK, there are over 40 venues set in extensive gardens or parklands that hold a wedding licence.

Alternatively, a good budget option is to hire a camping barn or a field and ask your friends to literally pitch up with drinks, food and tents. It's a good idea to also hire a barn in case of bad weather or at least have a pub nearby. Some campsites belong to farms, so bed and breakfast is often available for guests who don't like camping.

Barns If you like a bit of line-dancing, you could hire a barn for your wedding. There are over twenty with wedding licences, some in magnificent surroundings.

Farms Farms also conjure up country and western themes, offering a rural, isolated setting with plenty of privacy and space. There are over twenty farms with wedding licences around the UK.

Other unusual venues The London Eye has proved a popular choice among gay couples. Other unusual venues include a bingo hall in Cricklewood, North London; a brewery in Wrexham; mines in Somerset, Cornwall and Wales; Brighton Sea Life Centre; Fortnum and Mason in London; a part of Tower Bridge in London; and a vineyard in Surrey. At Denbies Wine Estate in Surrey, for example, your guests can enjoy a winery tour, cinema experience and tasting in the cellars. See www.gay-friendly-wedding-venues.com/unusualweddingvenues and www.civilvenues.com.

Use the Budget Planner on page 218 to record you final agreed amount and supplier.

Money-saving tips

- Hold your civil partnership on a weekday or outside the peak summer season, which is May to September.
- Hire a venue for the ceremony itself and hold the reception at home.
- Hire a venue only and either do your own catering or hire caterers.
- Find venues where you supply the booze.
- Hold the reception in a gay bar and ask people to pay for their own drinks.
- Invite only close friends and family to the ceremony and have a separate larger party later.

Questions to ask when you first contact a venue

- Is the venue licensed to carry out civil partnership ceremonies?
- Have they had a gay wedding before?
- What are the contact details for the nearest registrar?
- Is the venue available on the required date or selection of dates?
- Can they send you a brochure and price list?
- How many people can the venue accommodate for the ceremony and catering?
- How much overnight accommodation is available?
- How many car parking spaces are available?
- Can you hire the venue on an exclusive-use basis?
- Will there be other weddings on the same day?
- Can you make a provisional booking?
- When do you need to confirm?
- How much do you have to pay as a deposit?
- Does the venue have any special discount arrangements with local suppliers?
- Can you see sample menus?
- Are outside caterers allowed?
- If the venue is open to the public, when is it available for hire?
- What are the contingencies if the weather is bad?
- Where is the nearest public transport/airport, etc.?

- Do you have to pay extra for the hire of tables, chairs, linen, dance floors?
- Are there any restrictions (for example, no stilettos, no red wine, no children, no disabled access)?
- Can they give you ideas for themes or decoration from other weddings?
- Do you need to hire any technical equipment, such as lights or a PA system?

To get some idea of price, ask the following:

- Cost of room hire for ceremony
- Cost of room hire for catering
- Starting price for wedding packages – what does this include?
- Can you supply your own alcohol?
- If so, is there any corkage cost?
- Cost of a bottle of house white/red wine
- Cost of a bottle of house champagne
- Any minimum spend on catering
- Minimum cost of a sit-down meal per head
- Minimum cost of a buffet meal per head
- Cost of accommodation
- Any extra costs (for example, hire of cake stand and knife)
- Do prices include VAT?

More detailed questions before you book the venue

- Do they allow confetti to be thrown at the venue?
- Can you bring your own band or DJ?
- Do they allow candles to be lit in the reception room?
- Do they allow professional firework displays at their venue?
- Do they have landing permission if you want to arrive by helicopter, balloon or private jet?
- Do they offer the option of a marquee?
- Are there separate rooms provided for the wedding, reception, meal, evening reception?
- Is there a changing room provided for the day?
- What is the latest finishing time?

Questions to ask in the build-up towards the big day

- Does the venue supply any flowers or decoration?
- Can the venue provide someone to act as the master of ceremonies for the day?
- Does the venue have a Public Address (PA) system for speeches?
- When can suppliers have access to begin setting up the rooms, e.g. florists, decorators, DJ?
- Is there any crèche or babysitting facility?
- When does the reception room need to be cleared by?
- Is there somewhere safe to store presents?
- What is the checkout time from accommodation?
- Where are the best photo opportunities?

Organising a reception at home

If you are organising the reception at home, there are still quite a few things to think about. Here are some pointers.

Space If space is tight indoors and you have a garden big enough, why not have your wedding reception in a marquee? They don't need to look like boy scout tents – there are specialist companies that will decorate them in an Eastern, Moroccan, Spanish or even Bollywood style. Options include beautiful Arabian carpets, luxury cushions for lounging or dining, lanterns, lamps and shiny brass tables – saves you travelling abroad and creates a special atmosphere. Marquee companies often provide generators – they may be noisy, but you'll be glad of them.

Catering If you have outside caterers, when do they need to set up and will they clean up? If you are doing it yourself, do you have enough crockery, cutlery, glasses and fridge space? And who is going to help clear up? Can you ask friends and family to help?

Children Make sure they are fed and entertained and you have decided where you are happy for them to venture – you don't want to find your house turned upside down while you are celebrating in the garden.

Pets Do they need to be looked after for the day?

Furniture How is the furniture going to be arranged in the house? Are there enough chairs? Do you need to borrow some?

Flowers One big floral arrangement as people come into the house sets the scene.

Jo and Imelda do it at home

We had both been fighting for lesbian and gay equality, so for us it was partly about exercising our civil rights, but also about celebrating our relationship with family and friends, very publicly. We chose to have a civil partnership within the first three weeks of the law changing, to be a part of history.

We had just bought a new house and wanted it to be the venue for the party, so we hired a marquee for the garden. Our friends set up the marquee and a dance floor, and ran the disco, while another friend did the catering.

We were really excited about having everyone back to our new house, as some hadn't seen it before and it meant a lot to us to celebrate at home. Although there was snow on the ground, we managed to have a barbecue and people danced in the marquee. But preparing the house was a lot of work and we had to cut down half the garden, as the marquee was too big, so I would only recommend having a reception at home if you have a high threshold for stress. We organised it all in four months – I think that is the bare minimum. If I were doing it again, I would definitely have planned a holiday afterwards.

However, the whole day was really special, wonderful, and one of the most important days in my life.

Jo Clare, Chief Executive of Housing Association

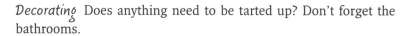

Decorating Does anything need to be tarted up? Don't forget the bathrooms.

Parking Contact neighbours to ask if driveways can be used or blocked.

Music See the section on music (pages 128–134), but warn your neighbours if you want to make a lot of noise.

Presents Find somewhere safe to keep them.

Lighting Check the lighting is suitable for the occasion.

Cleaning Arrange for a cleaner to come in before and after the event.

Speeches Where is a good place to make them?

Contingency plans What will you do if it rains and you were planning to use the garden, or if it's too hot and people need shade?

Decide on catering

There are three types of catering that you will want to consider for your wedding: self-catering, outside catering and in-house catering. The first can be done in your own home, or at a venue that you hire, such as a village hall or marquee. Outside caterers can be used in your own home or at any venue that allows them on their premises. However, most venues have their own in-house caterers, although they may allow you to supply the alcohol.

Alternatively, if you are having a very small reception, for up to ten friends, a good option is to book a table at a restaurant. To limit the budget, choose a set menu and specific wines ahead of time. Don't forget to have a vegetarian option.

When you get your estimates, keep them in a file or record in the

Budget Planner (Table 2 on pages 218–219), and then when you have decided on the best price and supplier, fill in the final column of the Budget Planner or online table.

Consider which of the following you would like:

- Canapés
- Buffet
- Sit-down meal
- Drinks
- Cakes
- Chocolate fountain(s)
- Ice sculpture
- Hire of catering paraphernalia

Contact caterers early on, as they will give you an idea of what you can get for your budget, and this might determine how many people you can invite. Apart from the food, there may well be a charge for linen, waiting staff and hire of equipment.

With regards to catering, it's important to think about the timing of your event. If you have a ceremony earlier in the day, you may have to feed people twice – once for lunch and then an evening buffet or meal. To save money, we held our ceremony at 4.30pm and the party started at 5.30pm. We had a reception first, serving pink Cava. We had thought about having canapés but I indulged my fantasy and had a chocolate fountain. Guests were able to dip strawberries, melon, pineapple, marshmallows and mini doughnuts into the flowing chocolate. After the drinks reception, which lasted an hour-and-a-half, we then had a substantial two-course buffet supper.

If you hold your ceremony in the late afternoon, people will have eaten lunch before they arrive. I have been to many a wedding where the ceremony starts at say 2.00pm, lasts an hour, then there are photographs and we finally eat at about 5.00pm. By that stage, people are either pissed, famished, or both – not a good combination.

- If using a caterer, insist on giving a deposit, no matter how small; it will make it harder for them to dump you should they be offered a larger function.
- Make sure you have the caterer's personal mobile phone number.
- Watch out for letters of recommendation that have the same handwriting – they could be a con.
- If visiting the kitchen of a caterer, satisfy yourself that it is clean.
- Ask for a tasting session and invite a few friends for second opinions.

If you want to really splash out, you can hire first-class chefs from top restaurants for the day. Special touches could include serving Beluga caviar, oysters and vintage champagne.

Canapés It is quite popular to have a canapé and champagne reception by itself, or as a preamble to the main meal. They can be very imaginative – my cousin, who had his civil partnership in Canada, brought a taste of England to the reception by having roast beef and Yorkshire pudding canapés.

Money-saving tip

- Jeremy Gibson, from Yumarooney caterers, says: 'If you are on a tight budget you should find a caterer who will do a "lay and leave" buffet and then rope in friends to help run the reception, thus avoiding staffing costs.'

Key questions

- What is the minimum and maximum number of guests you want to invite?
- What type of food do you want?
- Do you want a sit-down meal or a buffet?
- If you are having a lunchtime wedding, do you want a buffet for the evening?
- Does the venue have all its own crockery and tables?
- If hiring a marquee, do you need a separate catering tent?
- Are there cooking facilities for outside caterers at the venue?
- Do they have references that you can contact?
- Are there any 'extras' not on their quotation?
- How much and what type of liability insurance do they have?
- What are their billing terms and conditions?
- What are their contingency plans if they are ill on the day?

Sit-down meals versus buffets If you are having a sit-down meal for more than twenty people, this will usually involve a set three-course menu that you choose in advance. Sometimes a venue will allow a choice of two or three dishes per course, but you need to check this. Others will allow a choice, but will want your guests to decide in advance. Co-ordinating everyone's choice can be a bit of a nightmare, but if you are well organised, you can ask your guests for choices in an information sheet you send out with the invitation, which they can return when they reply. Don't forget to ask guests on the invitation for any dietary requirements, and if you are serving meat or fish, it is advisable to offer at least one vegetarian alternative.

Sit-down meals can be slightly cheaper than a buffet since the caterer only has to supply the food required and there is no choice. However, staffing will be more expensive than with a buffet. When Laura and I got quotations, the sit-down meal came in a pound cheaper than a buffet, but we wanted the occasion to be less formal and for people to have more choice. For the extra pound, guests had a selection of four main dishes, three salads and three puddings. There were also lots of extras such as dips, samosas and olives. We combined the best of both worlds as people had place settings at specific tables, rather than trying to stand around eating or grabbing chairs, and they could eat a wide range of food.

Sometimes people have a sit-down meal during the day and a finger buffet in the evening. Hotels will often provide an evening buffet quite cheaply if you have already had a main meal for your guests. With a buffet, make sure anyone with mobility problems has someone on hand to help them get their food.

If the buffet is your main meal, it is also quite a good idea to have the starter, or at least bread rolls, on the tables so that people have something to keep them going before their table is called to the buffet and don't have to queue for both courses.

Cheaper options If you are doing the catering yourself, have a buffet and ask friends and family to each bring a dish. Or ask one of your local restaurants, supermarkets, or bakers if they have a catering service for you in your own home or local venue, or perhaps they supply all the food ready prepared for you to reheat.

Drinks

If you have opted for self-catering or outside caterers, you will probably be supplying your own drinks. Even if you've chosen in-house catering, some venues allow you to provide drinks either for free or at a price per bottle, known as corkage. There can be different corkage prices for champagne and wine. Caterers make a big profit margin on alcohol, sometimes around 500 per cent, so if you are on a tight budget, supplying your own can save you a huge amount of money.

There are other ways to save money on booze – if you live near a Channel port, nip over to France for the day to stock up, but bear in mind that you need to factor in the cost of the travel and your time. Or keep an eye on supermarket websites for special offers. After Christmas, you can get some great deals on vintage wines. Tap in 'cheap wine' on Google, and a whole range of companies come up, from big name supermarkets to specialist wine retailers. You can also get price comparisons on sites such as kelkoo.co.uk. I would recommend a wine-tasting session before the big day to make sure you are happy with your selection.

Many of these companies offer free delivery, the loan of glasses (usually at around £1 deposit per glass), huge ice boxes to keep

- If you can store your wine, buy in the January sales; if not, buy in January and ask for a later delivery date.
- Take advantage of online wine retailers' discounts for first-time buyers. Ask friends and family to sign up and buy cases so you all get the discount.
- Buy sparkling wine or Cava instead of champagne – it is usually at least half the price.

18–24 bottles cool, three or four ice bags per box, and a sale or return policy. However, you need to return bottles in a saleable condition. If they've been floating in an ice bucket for four hours, the label might have fallen off, so be prepared to drink any leftovers – such a hardship.

Other drinks options On a more sober note, remember the teetotallers, children and drivers – they will need a plentiful supply of soft drinks and water. However, it is a good idea to check with parents of any young children attending, in case they don't want fizzy drinks readily available. You won't want a load of hyper kids running around, going crazy. A load of drunken adults running around – well, that's another matter . . .

For those who don't like wine, you may want to supply beer, or spirits and mixers. If this sounds a bit overwhelming, you can always have a bar facility. Obviously, some venues will have this anyway and you can either put a certain amount of money behind the bar or have a cash bar where people buy their own drinks. This is a good idea after the reception if people want to go on drinking into the night. One option is to tell guests that the first drink is on you, and then pick up the tab at the end of the event.

If you are holding your celebration at a venue without a bar, you can rent a bar facility complete with optics and barrels of beer. They come with or without staff. You can also supply your own alcohol or ask the rental company to provide it – they will provide all the equipment, a licence and staff. This is a good idea if you want to offer a wide range of spirits, for example.

If you do hire a bar, book as far in advance as possible. One supplier I spoke to, The Mobile Bar Company, already had orders for 2010 – now that's getting your drinks orders in. Because of other events requiring bars, busy times of year are the end of July, when there are summer fêtes and festivals, the beginning of August, and the first weekend in September. Saturdays are always the most popular day. A good option is a Sunday before a bank holiday – this gives everyone a chance to cure their hangover before going back to work.

Considerations when hiring a bar are the cost of mileage, access to the venue and parking. Some of the equipment is very heavy, so clambering up the steps of an ancient village hall can cause problems. Another potential problem, especially in a marquee, is electricity, so you might need to hire a generator. An extension lead from a house might not cope with a bar, lighting, disco and heated trays. You don't want to have to choose between dancing, drinking, eating or being able to see each other!

Things to check If you are supplying your own drinks or bringing an outside bar into a venue, check that they accept the type of drink you are proposing. Some stately homes with antique rugs or furniture won't accept red wine. Others may not allow draught beer. However, you may be able to get round it by putting down specialist matting, or serving drinks only in the marquee, even if the ceremony is in a stately home.

How much drink do you need In terms of quantity needed, it depends on how long your event will last, the temperature, salt content in food and the company you keep! The general guidance is to allow half a bottle of wine and half a bottle of bubbly per person and add some for those lushes of your acquaintance. People's preference for red or white wine is fairly evenly split, with white just having the edge, especially in the summer. If you don't want to offer an option, serve rosé, punch or a mulled wine and be done with it. You also need to allow about half a litre of water per person. A 75cl standard bottle of wine or bubbly holds five to six glasses. A 2-litre bottle of water has seven to nine servings. Our caterer told us a neat trick: buy 20 bottles of posh water to go on the tables to start with and then fill them up from the tap during the course of the evening. No one will be any the wiser. He also said not to bother with sparkling water, as most people could cope with still and his tap trick wouldn't be so convincing!

Think through the day and work out how much you need of different types of drink. Go through your guest list and work out how many are big drinkers or teetotallers. It is a good idea to buy on a sale or return basis unless you have plenty of space at home and the urge to carry on drinking after the party! Also allow for glass breakage or people losing their glasses. To give you an idea, a typical shopping list of drinks is set out on pages 84-85. This is based on drinks required for an afternoon reception followed by a sit-down dinner and then dancing until midnight, and caters for 100 people.

Catering paraphernalia

If you are thinking about self-catering or using outside caterers, you may be overwhelmed by the amount of equipment that is needed, and what can seem like a cheap price for food can soon begin to

Money-saving tips

- Don't open a load of bottles and put them on tables – you might end up with a lot of half-finished bottles.
- Ask the waiting staff to keep topping people's glasses up, or replacing finished bottles.
- If you don't have staff, set up a table with bottles available and corkscrews – people will soon come and help themselves.
- If you are inviting some people just for the evening, don't ask them to buy a present, suggest they just bring a bottle.

Drinks calculator

	Bottles
Champagne reception	
allowing 2–3 glasses champagne each	50
Soft drinks options, allowing 1 serving each	12 x 2 litres
Orange juice or sparkling water (if required)	
Dinner	
allowing ½ bottle of wine each	25 red and 25 white
Soft drinks options, allowing 2 servings each	24 x 2 litres
Orange juice, sparkling (if required) and still water and lemonade	
After dinner toast	
allowing 1 glass each	
Sparkling wine	20
Drinking into the night	
allowing 2 glasses each	20 red and 20 white
Soft drinks options, allowing 2 servings each	24 x 2 litres
Beers, allowing 50 servings	50 x 33cl bottles

Top tip

Add cold water to your ice buckets or boxes to speed up the cooling process. Wine will take only about ten minutes to chill down in an ice bucket.

Shopping list

50 bottles of champagne

45 bottles of red wine

45 bottles of white wine

20 bottles of sparkling wine (if required)

60 x 2-litre bottles of soft drinks

50 x 33cl bottles of beer

Glasses

120 champagne flutes – 240 if you don't have anyone to wash them between the initial reception and the toast.

120 tumblers

120 wine glasses

120 tall glasses for juice

Ice boxes: 11 if you want to keep everything chilled from the start, or you could halve this if you have people available to keep refilling the boxes

Ice: 33 ice bags for 11 boxes

Ice buckets for tables: 10 if you have ten tables

Ice: 10 bags for ice buckets

Corkscrews, bottle top cutters and bottle openers: 10 of each would be handy

Boxes to contain empties: you can use the crates the bottles came in and recycle them.

mount up once everything else is added on. Here are some of the things to think about.

- Main plates
- Side plates
- Pudding bowls
- Glasses
- Dinner knife
- Dinner fork
- Dinner spoon
- Butter knife
- Dessert spoons and forks
- Serving spoons
- Serving platters
- Serving bowls
- Juice jugs
- Trays
- Trestle table
- Linen for trestle table
- Linen for dining tables
- Napkins
- Corkscrews
- Cake knife
- Cake stand
- Bottle bin
- Large ice bags
- Temporary oven and hob
- Hot plates
- Temporary refrigeration
- Tables
- Chairs
- Chair covers and bows
- Temporary flooring

When you are hiring equipment, find out the policies on damage, costs of delivery, and when you have to return everything that you've hired. You'll probably have to pay a hefty deposit.

Top tip

For a special touch, have napkins monogrammed with your names and the date of your wedding.

Sweet and tasty things

I love the symbolism of seeing a traditional wedding cake with two men or two women on the top tier. You can be even more radical and have a cake designed in a wide range of shapes, including a woman in bondage. If you don't want a cake, how about a chocolate fountain, or a stack of cheese?

When you get your estimates keep them in a file or record in the Budget Planner (Table 2 on pages 218–219), then, when you have decided on the best price and supplier, fill in the final column of the Budget Planner. You can also download the table from www.gay-friendly-wedding-venues.com/budget.

Cakes Think about the type of cake you want, because some cakes, especially fruit or alcohol-soaked varieties, are better if they are prepared up to a year in advance and you'll need to order it.

If you are not keen on traditional wedding cakes, which are basically fruit cakes with marzipan and icing, have a three-tiered cake with different flavours on each level. Or have individual cup cakes, arranged on a tiered stand.

Co-ordinate your cake with your colour scheme, theme or season, or choose something personal or amusing. Jane Asher's Party Cakes and Sugarcraft company has been supplying cakes to the gay community for years, and has even made a cake of two women in bondage. Other cakes the company has produced for same-sex couples include two female cats, dressed up as brides, and one with models of the two men getting married.

If you don't have a sweet tooth, for something different order huge slabs of cheese layered like a cake, as chef Allegra McEvedy so famously did. There's even a company that specialises in this: www.teddingtoncheese.co.uk

Make sure you buy cake toppers of two brides or two grooms.

Allegra and Susi conjure up a flamboyant feast

Allegra McEvedy, co-founder of Leon restaurants and cookery writer, says she and her partner, Susi Smither, a party organiser, primarily decided to marry because they plan to have children and want to create a stable environment for them. 'We also both like a good party and have always thought that gay couples have just as much right to their big day as heteros.'

They held their partnership ceremony in a registry office, and then, two days later, following a blessing in a church, they had a celebration at the Weir Bank in Bray, a riverside venue. Allegra explains: 'We always wanted to do our own thing and for us, three courses, buffets and substantial canapés had all been done to death. So we came up with the idea of Trolleys and Dollies. The Dollies were girls walking around with usherette trays filled with Mrs King's pork pies, warm crab tartlets, or other bits of deliciousness. And the Trolleys were like overgrown dim sum vehicles winding their way through the guests. One trolley had whole sirloins of roast beef with watercress and horseradish; another had two soups served from huge china tureens. Another had whole sides of the best smoked salmon, while yet others had bales of English asparagus with hollandaise or melted butter. We had a guy from the local Chinese restaurant who shredded Peking duck for pancakes and we also brought in expert sushi makers who rolled to order at each table. Ham stands with Pata Negra circled while Southern Fried chicken and ham biscuits (a nod to Susi's Virginian parentage) also worked the crowd.'

Their cake was also completely different. 'Neither of us really likes wedding cake and we both have a bit of a passion for cheese, so during one drunken wedding meeting at Leon Ludgate, a bunch of us came up with the idea of The Cheese Cake. A few days later our best man, Fred, duly went off and spent a very happy afternoon at Neal's Yard flirting over the ewe's milk. Eleven cheeses and a thousand pounds later we had the most beautiful towering stack, from an enormous Montgomery's Cheddar wheel at the bottom up to the tiny pyramid-shaped goat's cheese, Tymsboro, at the top.'

Allegra's advice is that if you really care about food, don't settle for anything less than amazing. Go in with your own ideas and don't let caterers push you towards salmon and chicken (with pasta for the veggies). It's your day and you deserve better than that.

- Order a large iced cake from your local bakery and don't tell them it's for a wedding – you'll be amazed at the price difference.
- Order a plain iced cake and make it look more expensive by decorating it with fresh or silk flowers, or topping it with strawberries.
- Make your own cake and then have it iced professionally.
- Serve the cake instead of dessert, or have a dessert and no cake.
- If you want the cake to look grand and have three or four tiers, but you don't need to feed that many people, a professional trick is to cut a block of polystyrene and ice it for the bottom layer – just don't serve it!

Chocolate fountains Chocolate fountains are very popular for functions and some hire companies have orders two years in advance, so book as early as possible.

The options for your wedding are:

- Hire a chocolate fountain company with staff to work the machine.
- Hire the machine and operate it yourself (known as 'dry hire').
- Buy your own chocolate fountain(s).

Some chocolate fountain companies will only host the fountain themselves, as they want to manage and look after the equipment. Apparently, there is a lot of skill involved in making sure the chocolate flows smoothly.

The chocolate fountain companies usually supply a range of fruit, such as pineapples, bananas, kiwi and strawberries, or marshmallows or fudge, on skewers to dip into the chocolate. Sometimes dipping food is charged per person or included in the hire price.

The fountains come in different sizes and can cater for between 30 and 300 people. You need to supply access to electricity and a table for each one. Make sure you don't stand them on a precious table or tablecloth, as there are bound to be drips.

If you have a large number of guests, it may be advisable to have two or three fountains on different tables to avoid unseemly bundles or long queues. A round table, with access all around, is the best option. It is also advisable to serve children rather than leaving them to help themselves, so that they don't make a huge mess.

Things to check

- Does the venue allow chocolate fountains?
- Do the staff of the hire company serve people, or just monitor the machine?
- Does the company bring a base, or do you need to provide a table?
- Does the company provide dipping food and, if so, what is it?
- Does the company provide napkins or plates?
- Do the operators have health and hygiene certificates?
- Does the company have public liability insurance?

Warning

If you are paying per person, watch out for companies that supply the food already skewered, or cut it in half, as this means you get less to dip than you would from a company that displays, for example, the whole strawberries for you to skewer and dip.

Book the registrar

You can tie the knot at a registry office, or any wedding venue in the UK that has a civil wedding licence, but wherever you decide to hold your ceremony, you have to 'give notice' of your intention to have a civil partnership at your *local* registry office. The earliest you can give notice to the registry office is one year in advance, although you can usually book a provisional date if you want to book further in advance. If you are in a real hurry, the minimum requirement is a 15-day notice period. Even if you want to elope to Scotland and you fancy the romance of marrying in Gretna Green, you still need to allow 15 clear days before you can tie the knot.

In England and Wales, you must make an appointment with the registrar (which may take a few weeks to arrange). You will both be interviewed separately and your details are then filled in online in a system called Ron – Registration online, which means that all registry offices have access to the information.

In Scotland, you can download an application form from the Internet and send the required details by post. You can also apply by post in Northern Ireland. This means you don't have to meet the registrar ahead of your ceremony in Scotland or Northern Ireland – you can just turn up on the day. However, I would advise meeting the registrar who is going to conduct your ceremony, so you are not complete strangers on such an important day. You can go through the details of the ceremony, and they will also be able to advise you on details such as the best places for people to stand to give readings or how to make a grand entrance.

Registry offices usually have a range of ceremony rooms for varying sizes of parties. These may include a small room with space for you and a couple of witnesses, through to the rooms where the council holds civic events.

You can find out where your local registry office is by visiting:

in England and Wales: www.gro.gov.uk
in Scotland: www.gro-scotland.gov.uk/files/civil-partnership-in-scotland.pdf
and in Northern Ireland: www.groni.gov.uk/index.htm

At least two weeks before your ceremony, the registry office will publish the details on its notice boards. These include your name, date of birth, marital status, occupation, nationality and where the civil partnership will take place. However, unlike for straight couples, and to prevent any potential homophobia, they don't include your address. In England, Wales and Northern Ireland, once you have given notice it is valid for twelve months, so if you want a big lead-up, or still need some time to think about it, you have some breathing space. However, in Scotland you have to get your act together, as you have only three months.

(See also Finding a venue, page 60.)

What paperwork do you need to give notice?

You need to take along two pieces of identity – ideally one should be your passport and another proving where you live.

If you're divorced, you also need to provide the decree absolute.

If you've already had a civil partnership dissolved, you must take along the final order of dissolution. If you've mislaid the paperwork, you can contact the court where the divorce or dissolution took place, or contact The Principal Registry of the Family Division (see the Directory of Useful Resources, page 203).

If your former husband, wife or civil partner has died, you should take along their death certificate.

What if one of us is subject to immigration controls?

If you are subject to immigration controls, you must give notice of your intention to register a civil partnership at one of the designated 76 registry offices in England and Wales (details on www.gro.gov.uk). All registry offices in Scotland and Northern Ireland are designated.

You need to meet one of the criteria detailed on pages 27–28.

How much does the ceremony and partnership certificate cost?

See pages 25–26 for details of the various fees involved. These may vary depending on the day of the week you are holding your ceremony and how far the registrar has to travel – if you're having the ceremony at a licensed venue rather than the local registry office. When you get your estimates, keep them in a file or record in the Budget Planner (Table 2 on page 218), then, when you have decided on the best price and supplier, fill in the final column of the Budget Planner. You can also download the table from www.gay-friendly-wedding-venues.com/budget.

Special circumstances

See page 29 for details of the circumstances where a) the 15-day waiting period does not apply, and b) you can register a civil partnership at a place other than a licensed venue.

What else do we need?

You need to have decided on the date of your civil partnership ceremony, even if you haven't yet chosen the venue. You may want to research venues before confirming the date (see Finding a venue, page 60), but you can change the date with the registrar if circumstances change.

What happens if one of us changes their mind?

If you change your mind about going through with the ceremony, after you have given notice, you need to write to the registrar. However, you will lose any fees paid.

What actually happens on the big day of signing?

You can either sign on the dotted line, 'the civil partnership schedule', in front of two witnesses, or you can make it into more of a ceremony. Camden registry office sent us four different options for the wording of the ceremony, all bound in a specially designed brochure. The words were much more romantic than I had expected. You can choose to amend the wording as long as it's agreed with the registrar ahead of time. You can also add readings, poetry or pieces of music (see the Directory of Useful Resources, page 205).

Key points to note are:

- Readings or poetry must have no religious connections or connotations.
- Photographs are normally taken *after* the ceremony.
- Video or audio recordings can be done throughout the ceremony with the agreement of the registrar.
- In our case, there were two registrars, but sometimes there is only one.

Although the Civil Partnership Act prevents any religious service from taking place during the registration of a civil partnership, there are gay-friendly clergy who are willing to travel the length and breadth of the country to give you a blessing after the event, although this can't take place at the registry office. For more information, see Celebrants, page 143, and the Directory of Useful Resources, page 205.

Top tips

- Book the registrar as soon as possible.
- Remember to give notice at your *local* registry office even if you want to marry somewhere else.
- Don't forget you need two witnesses.
- Think about how you can make the ceremony personal.

4 Forward thinking

This chapter covers a few key elements of administration that you need to set in motion ahead of your partnership ceremony. Some of them might seem a bit serious in amongst the fun parts of planning your big day, but they are well worth thinking about to make sure your finances are secure. Others are more fun, such as planning your honeymoon and deciding on wedding stationery.

Legal and financial considerations

It might be a bit of a shock to bring you from chocolate fountains to finance and administration, but there are some key actions to take ahead of your wedding day. For example, once you have a civil partnership ceremony your existing Will becomes null and void; also, if you don't take out wedding insurance you risk losing a lot of money if the unforeseen happens. You may also want to seek advice from accountants and lawyers if one or both of you own their own property. If you are changing your name, another consideration is the need to inform all the relevant people, banks, etc. (See also Frequently asked questions, pages 24–29.)

Wills

Make sure your Wills are up to date. Any previous Will becomes invalid when you have a civil partnership, unless you have written a Will with provision for such an event. In this case, you need to specify the date of your intended civil partnership.

Wedding insurance

Once you start to shell out money on deposits for the venue and other suppliers, I strongly advise you, for peace of mind in the run-up and on the day itself, to take out wedding insurance. Cover starts from around £50. If the wedding or reception has to be cancelled or even cut short due to reasons out of your control, the insurer will pay, depending on your level of cover, some or all of the following: all deposits and other charges due, or already paid, relating to transport, catering, accommodation, photographs, flowers and dress hire.

Cover can also include cancellation due to severe weather conditions (pluvius insurance), if this means that the majority of guests can't reach your wedding. It also pays for alternative transport if the driver and car you've booked doesn't turn up.

It will usually cover loss of wedding rings, stolen presents, photographs going wrong, or delayed travel on your honeymoon. The top five claims are wedding attire damaged, having to re-take the wedding photos, cancellation of the wedding due to an illness or bereavement, caterers not turning up, and loss of wedding rings.

Name change

If one of you wants to change their name to their partner's, you can do this after the civil partnership, by using your civil partnership certificate as proof of your new status.

If you want to change your name before the ceremony – so that travel documents and passports have your new name – you need to do it in advance by deed poll.

If you want to change your name to form a double-barrelled version of both your surnames, you also have to do this by deed poll. For further information, visit www.ukdps.co.uk. You can apply online at www.ukdps.co.uk – it is quick and easy. You will also need to apply for a new passport, so allow time for this.

Ownership of homes

You should seek legal and financial advice about property owner-ship to see if it is advantageous to become tenants in common, or to find other ways in which to simplify your financial and property arrangements.

Pensions and life insurance

You should check any pensions or employment and life insurance schemes you hold to make sure that your partner is named as the beneficiary of any survivor pension or life insurance payouts. Make a note to inform all relevant financial institutions of your new sta-tus of civil partners, shortly after your ceremony. If you are going away for a long honeymoon, ask a friend or family member to post out the letters for you.

Book your honeymoon

After all the hard work of organising a civil partnership, you deserve a break. Even if you are on a tight budget, try to have a weekend away locally. You may want to postpone your honeymoon for a week or so if people have travelled from abroad for your wedding – it's a shame not to see more of them.

If you want to have a romantic time and not worry about being stared at or hassled, go for a gay-friendly destination. These include:

UK: Brighton, Bournemouth, Manchester, Blackpool,
Torquay, London.

US: Key West, Florida; New York City; Provincetown,
Massachusetts; Santa Fe, New Mexico; Chicago; Las Vegas;
California; Hawaii.

Canada: Toronto, Vancouver.

European cities: Amsterdam, Berlin, Paris, Prague.

Greece: Lesbos, Mykonos.

Spain: Gran Canaria, Sitges, Ibiza, Fuerteventura, Majorca, Benidorm, Torremolinos,

Australia and New Zealand: particularly Sydney and Auckland.

South Africa: particularly Cape Town.

Danny Waine, at travel agents Perfect Gay Honeymoons, says popular choices for women are Key West in Florida, the Greek island of Lesbos, and Provincetown in Massachusetts.

'For men, we generally find Gran Canaria is a popular choice throughout the summer, being replaced by South Africa and New Zealand during the winter.'

Multi-centre holidays are becoming more popular, particularly for 'once-in-a-lifetime' honeymoon bookings. This might involve round-the-world trips with stop-offs in New York, Las Vegas, California, Thailand, or Singapore and then on to Australia or New Zealand for some beach relaxation. Why not time your trip to coincide with Sydney's Mardi Gras or other Gay Pride events around the world?

The most important thing to think about is how you picture your ideal honeymoon, but in realistic surroundings. Danny warns: 'Unfortunately, some people see the Maldives' sandy beaches and imagine cuddling up by the sea, but in reality this is not something that would go down well with the host community.' It's really important to get advice and to research places that are gay-friendly.

The UK's Foreign and Commonwealth Office doesn't give a list of countries to avoid, but warns same-sex couples to check guidebooks, the Internet or embassies to find out about different countries' attitudes. It advises: 'In some countries same-sex relationships are illegal and punishable by imprisonment, or even the death penalty. You should check attitudes towards same-sex relationships in the country you plan to visit, and exercise caution where unsure. Gay, lesbian, bisexual and transgender travellers may have particular difficulties in countries where a large percentage of the population have strongly held religious beliefs which have traditionally been opposed to same-sex relationships.' It also advises people to head for cities, rather than rural locations. (See: www.fco.gov.uk)

Vicky Stirling, of travel agents Farside Africa, suggests: 'If couples want to go to places like Africa, South America, or Asia, speak to specialist companies who deal with these countries to check how gay-friendly they are.'

If you want to go the whole hog, many top-class hotels offer honeymoon packages. There are stunning five-star hotels that will do everything they can to make your honeymoon as special as possible – limousine transfers, champagne on arrival, spa treatments, whatever money will buy.

If you want to book a honeymoon suite in a particular hotel, it's worth making enquiries as soon as possible so that the room can be reserved. Danny advises booking the honeymoon six to nine months before departure. He adds: 'I would definitely make it clear to your agent that you are going on honeymoon. From my experience it has never led to a more expensive holiday, but failing to do so can lead to you missing out on many benefits that honeymoon couples receive.' He also recommends pointing out that you are a same-sex honeymoon couple. 'This is to ensure that the tour operator and hotel extend the benefits to same-sex couples.'

Decide on wedding stationery

There's more to wedding stationery than meets the eye and, for consistency, it is best to have all printed material designed at the

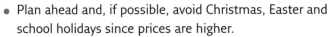

Top tips

- Plan ahead and, if possible, avoid Christmas, Easter and school holidays since prices are higher.
- Combine your honeymoon with marrying abroad (see Marrying abroad, pages 31–33).
- Some tour operators run wedding gift lists, so family and friends can contribute to the cost of your honeymoon.
- If you want privacy, hire a secluded villa.
- Remember to book appointments for any necessary inoculations and obtain relevant visas.
- See the Directory of Useful Resources, page 205, for travel contacts.
- When you get your estimates fill them in on Table 2 Budget Planner, pages 220, and then when you have decided on your honeymoon, fill in the final column of the plan, or on the table you have downloaded from www.gay-friendly-wedding-venues.com/budget.

same time. If you want to go to town, you can have all the following items:

- 'Save the date' cards
- Invitations
- Information for guests
- Reply cards
- Order of the day sheets
- Order of ceremony sheets
- Evening invitations
- Name cards
- Menu cards

- Table plans
- Table numbers
- Guest book
- Favour boxes
- Wedding album
- Thank you cards

Also, if you can afford it, you might like to have tissue pouches designed in the same way as your stationery, and hand out tissues as guests arrive.

Options include buying standard pre-printed stationery in a shop or online, having bespoke stationery designed and then printed or handmade, or making your own. You also need to think about the type, colour and size of paper.

The stationery can be designed to co-ordinate with your wedding theme, or you could make it very personal and have it all printed with a caricature or photograph of both of you. Another popular option is to incorporate gay symbols (see pages 59–60).

'Save the date' cards

Once you've fixed the date of your wedding and have booked the registry office and venue for that day, it's a good idea to send out 'save the date' cards. This will enable guests to mark the date in their diary and, if necessary, make travel arrangements. If you want to co-ordinate these with the rest of your stationery, you need to start planning now. It also means you don't have to immediately rush around gathering all the information you need for the invitation, such as accommodation options and maps, but that you are able to tell people the date well in advance – meaning they will be more likely to be able to attend. The cards can be designed in the same way as your invitations. Alternatively, buy standard cards, or make your own. If you don't want to send out these cards, at the

Top tip

When you tell people about the date, you may want to ask them to accept a specific role, such as a witness (you need two), best man or best woman, or to give a reading or speech, but don't rush into this – it can be planned nearer the time. (See Choosing readings, speakers and other roles for friends and family, page 177.) Make sure you pick responsible and reliable people to have key roles. If you want them to wear specific outfits, you also have to build in time for this.

very least, I would recommend an e-mail or phone call to prospective guests informing them of the date, especially to people who live far away.

Invitations

The invitation sets the tone of your wedding and should reflect the ideas that came from your wish list (see pages 216–217). Having compiled this, you will know if you want your civil partnership to be formal, fun, posh or homespun.

Numbers Work out how many invitation cards you need, rather than counting the number of guests you have coming. It sounds obvious, but it is an easy mistake to think you've got 80 guests and assume you need 80 invitations, when many will be couples or families. Allow for a few extra cards in case you make mistakes when you are filling in the names, or if you get refusals and want to invite other people. But remember that other stationery, such as order of ceremony sheets, should be calculated on the number of guests.

Wording Traditionally, an invitation would say: *'hosts' names* [which may be parents] request the pleasure of *guests' names* to attend the wedding on date, time, place, etc.'. It is probably a rare occasion when parents are paying for a civil partnership, but if this is the case, you may want to include them on the invitation in a more informal way. For example: 'Joanne and Mary, along with their parents, would like to invite...'

You also need to include, either on the invitation or on a separate insert, essential information such as the date, time, address of venue for ceremony and reception, directions by road and public transport, parking arrangements, dress code, local accommodation, address for RSVP, mobile phone number for emergencies on the day, dietary requirements, latest date for RSVPs, and gift list details. Also make it clear if children are invited. (See also Send out invitations, page 176.)

You may want to employ a professional calligrapher to write the invitations, and then you won't have to worry that your writing won't match up to the standard of the stationery. Remember to factor in the time needed for this.

Design If you want handmade or bespoke stationery, there is a wide range of gay-friendly designers (see the Directory of Useful Resources, page 205, for contacts). If you decide on a bespoke design, sit down with the designer and look at previous examples of their work. Be honest about what you like and dislike, so that they can build up an idea of your tastes. It is a good idea to go armed with a large sheet of paper displaying images you have cut out from magazines, showing the colours and styles that appeal to you – this is sometimes known as a mood board. If you do create one, it will also be useful if you are having other elements of your civil partnership designed, such as outfits and even the decoration for the room. Ideas range from invitations cut into a shape to represent your theme to an invitation wrapped up in a scroll and even placed in a bottle.

Once you have agreed on the design elements with your stationer, they should prepare a few samples for your approval.

If you engage a designer, they ideally need two to three months to take your brief, show you proofs, finalise the design and either handmake the stationery or send them to print. Although, you can always get things done quickly if you're in a hurry. Some stationers I spoke to could turn an invitation around in five days, but at a premium.

If you want to make your invitations very personal, ask a good photographer or caricaturist to take a portrait of you both to include on the front. Another idea is to hint at your professions or hobbies, such as by combining, for example, two stethoscopes in the shape of a heart, or by using musical symbols.

Stationery designer Helen Eason, of Red Nell Designs, says: 'Many people assume that handmade wedding stationery is more expensive than mass-produced printed cards, available from high street stationers. This is not necessarily the case and the major benefit of choosing handmade over printed is the client has full input into colour scheme, design layout, wording, and so on.'

If you want to make your own stationery, there are a number of websites and shops that sell all the accessories, such as templates, handmade paper, ribbons and trimming. For a special touch, you could dry flowers and stick them on the invitations, or use ribbon or material to tie a bow, as in tying the knot, and stick that on the front.

Invitation on a CD or DVD If you want something completely different, send out a CD or DVD invitation. You can buy or download from the Internet the software that enables you to create CDs or DVDs with a personalised introduction, including photographs of you and set to your favourite music, etc. When your

'Always ask to see a sample of your invitation in your chosen colour theme before you commit to any order,' says Donna Newton of Donna Michelle Designs. She also highly recommends asking for a paper copy of the design. If it is sent through by e-mail, the fonts may change when you download them unless they are in pdf format. Even in pdf format, the colour may not be truly representative. 'Having it on paper allows you to check closely for any errors and to see the layout before it goes to print,' she says.

guests insert the CD or DVD into their computers, they can access all the information that would have been on a printed invitation. This is particularly useful for links to local accommodation and travel directions.

Reply cards Reply cards are enclosed with the invitations and are pre-printed with a space both for people to accept or decline the invitation, and to add their name. These are a good idea because the guests will have the means to respond quickly – people often leave replying to the last minute, especially when confronted with the thought of having to purchase a card to send back.

Order of the day

The order of the day sheets are generally a timetable of the event, which you either hand out when people arrive, or post ahead of time, so they know when different parts of the celebrations start. People feel more comfortable knowing what to expect, and this can be particularly useful if you have any gaps between the ceremony and reception or evening function.

Order of ceremony

Order of ceremony sheets are usually more detailed than the order of the day, and can be a full transcript of the ceremony, including readings, vows, music, etc. You can make them into a souvenir of the day with a photograph of you both on the front, for example. I think this is a really lovely idea, as the words people say to each other are often very moving and it is nice to be able to read them again at a later stage. Laura and I printed the detail of the ceremony on pink paper and rolled into a scroll, then tied it all together with pink ribbon.

Evening invitations

These can be more informal, but make sure you include useful information such as local accommodation, transport, parking, etc. Also make sure the start time allows for all the daytime activities, such as speeches, to be over. I heard of one straight wedding where all the evening guests were kept waiting outside for half-an-hour while the speeches finished. They certainly felt like second-class citizens.

Name cards

If you are having a table plan with assigned seats, you will need name cards so that people know where to sit. Again, these can replicate the motif of your invitations on a smaller scale. You may also want to use a calligrapher or handwriting font to make them look special. Think about the rest of the table decoration and make sure the design of your table stationery complements it. An alternative is to have a table plan with names assigned to a table but not dictating who sits next to whom. This does speed things up, but I think it's better to decide in advance who sits next to each other – you generally know who will get on best. When you give the name cards to the caterers, make sure that they are in order and separated out for each table, so that the catering staff are not spending hours cross-referencing with the table plan.

Menu cards

These detail the food and wine to be served. It's a good way to whet your guests' appetites, and descriptions of food often make the menu sound very luxurious. You can also add a bit of history about why you chose the wine. For example, we picked a white New Zealand wine from an area where we'd had a wonderful holiday. Your venue or caterer may supply menu cards free of charge, so check this before you get them printed. Usually, two or three per table will suffice, but you might want to give each guest their own personal menu, which is either laid on their plate or wrapped in their napkin.

Table plans

If you are using a table plan (see Table plans, pages 189–191), design it to complement the design of other stationery, or have a photograph of you both in the middle. Again, you could use a calligrapher to make this look special. Make sure the plan is big enough for people to read if they are standing around in a crowd of, say, ten people – you need at least A2 size paper. It is a good idea to have two copies of it made for display, so people can find their table quickly. You can also type up lists of guests for each table and just have the plan showing where the tables are situated. (You will probably want to leave filling in the names on the plan to the last week before the party, in case anyone drops out.) There are specialist companies, such as www.thetableplanner.com, who will design plans with a twist – for example, in the style of a poster for a Hollywood film or the line-up for a rugby match.

Table numbers

These need to be prominently displayed on each table so that people can find their tables easily. The venue may supply them, but if not, you can again incorporate your motif into their design.

Guest book

The point of a guest book is that people can write messages to you about the day, or their good wishes for your future. Often the book is passed from table to table after the main meal has been served, or it can be left by the cake table for people to add in their comments. You may want a trusted friend to start it off so they set the tone and indicate to others the kind of messages you want. If you aren't buying a ready-made book, this is another item of stationery you can have printed to complement your theme.

- Check whether the venue has its own wedding stationery – it might be included in the price of your wedding package.
- Print the menu on your seating plan.
- Combine your order of ceremony and order of the day sheets.
- Add a name-tag to your favour boxes so they double up as name cards.
- If stationers are designing or printing the whole range of items you require, ask for bulk discounts.
- Use white card – coloured card is always more expensive.
- Choose a standard size – for example A5, which is A4 folded in half.

Top tips

- Check proofs of your stationery very carefully and ask someone else to give them a second read. Sometimes it is easier to spot mistakes if you read proofs backwards from the last word to the first; that way, you read each word separately.
- If you are making your own stationery, don't forget to order envelopes.
- Even if some family members or friends have indicated that they won't be able to attend, it is a courtesy to inform them of your wedding.
- It's a good idea to have a list or spreadsheet of guests' names so that you can tick them off when they reply and add in any details about dietary requirements.

Favour boxes

Again, favour boxes can match the general theme of the day. These boxes were traditionally only for female guests, but this seems a bit sexist. They are supposed to contain a little keepsake of the day and are often filled with sweets. See the section on Decorations and floral displays, pages 148–158, for more detail.

Wedding album

You can buy beautiful albums with handmade paper, or ask your stationer to design an album to match your other stationery. Make sure you aren't duplicating the services offered by your photographer.

Thank you cards

Continuing the theme, order thank you cards from your stationer, or buy them pre-printed. Another option is to choose a photograph from your wedding to stick on the front.

Questions to ask your stationer/designer

- What is the minimum order?

- How much do extras cost?

- How much is the deposit and when is final payment due?

- How many versions of designs are produced in the price before you decide on the final version?

- Is there a delivery charge?

- Are envelopes included in the price?

- Decide who is taking responsibility for the items you require. When you get your estimates fill them in on Table 2 Budget Planner, pages 219–220, and then when you have chosen your supplier, fill in the final column of the plan, or on the table you have downloaded from www.gay-friendly-wedding-venues.com/budget.

Look into gift lists

This may seem a bit premature, but you want to start thinking about a gift list in order to include information with your invitation. Gift lists are also known as wedding lists or wedding registry in the US. There are various options for your lists:

- Items at a specific store, such as John Lewis
- Gift vouchers for specific shops, or online stores such as Amazon
- Items from a range of suppliers or shops
- Specific amounts to pay for elements of your honeymoon
- Donations to charity
- Handmade or homemade presents

Gift lists at department stores

The traditional route is to set up a gift list with a department store, such as John Lewis, Harrods, Debenhams or Argos. The shops offer a free gift list service and you can either set them up in person or do it online.

Department stores recommend setting up gift lists about ten weeks before the event, so that the product range is the same when your gifts are purchased. However, you can always add things to your list under their 'manage your list' options. Some of them, like John Lewis, operate the list six weeks before your wedding and two weeks after, so you should check this with each store. They also offer the option of gift vouchers, so if you want more expensive items, people can contribute to them. Another way to deal with expensive items is to divide them up into £10 chunks, so that people buy contributions towards a flat screen TV, or whatever budget-buster items you've chosen.

Your guests can buy over the phone, online or in the shop, but they sometimes need a code or password to access your gift list. They can tell the gift list department their price range and will be told what is available, so they can make a selection. It's also important that guests let the gift list department of a store know if they buy something in the shop, so it's deleted from the list.

You should also check whether items will be wrapped or just packaged up. Usually, they are packaged up for safe transport, rather than individually wrapped. Most stores will deliver all the presents free of charge, but make sure you arrange a date when you are back from your honeymoon. Usually, deliveries are collated three weeks after your wedding because they may have to order some items if they are out of stock. They will also wait until the list has closed before ordering all items within a range, to avoid slight variations in fabrics or tones of pottery, for example.

Some shops also offer you a gift voucher for setting up your gift list and others will add a percentage to money pledged by your guests if your gifts are over a certain amount – for example, some will add 3 per cent if your gifts come to more than £1,000 in total.

Top tips

- It is a good idea to set up your gift list before sending out your invitations, since you can then enclose information about how to purchase gifts. Some department stores will print inserts for your invitations as part of the service.
- You can usually view the progress of your list online.
- Check the store's returns policy, as some will only allow you to return 25 per cent of your gifts, which is fair enough, since you chose them in the first place.
- Find out what happens if your guests don't contribute enough for an item on your list. Some stores will allow you to top it up, or transfer the money to another gift, or get a refund of the cash.
- Check how gift list operators make their money – i.e. if they charge a percentage of your gifts, or take money from suppliers, etc.
- Check what happens if your wedding is cancelled or postponed.
- Choose a range of items from the frivolous to the practical and at different prices.

Gift lists from a range of suppliers and shops

You can also create wedding gift lists with companies that specialise in this area. They offer a wide range of gifts from different suppliers including designer ranges. Here is a selection:

www.weddingshop.com: this has a range of 250 brands of mainly household items.

www.wrapit.co.uk: over 350 brands from garden furniture to books and electrical goods.

www.marriagegiftlist.com: allows you to compile a list from a range of department stores, so you are not limited to one shop.

www.theweddinglist.com: this is the General Trading Company's site, which sources products from around the world, offering a wide selection of glass and chinaware, contemporary and traditional furniture, oriental and African artefacts, and kitchenware.

Gay lists

If you want specifically gay presents, you can set up a gift list with lavendarlifestyles.co.uk, which has a wide range of lesbian and gay art, jewellery, homeware, books and videos.

Alternative lists

There is a growing number of alternative gift lists. For example, www.thebottomdrawer.co.uk will host lists for people who want a garden makeover, new kitchen, or hot tub in the bathroom. It has a network of skilled suppliers who will work with you to decide on what you want in your home and then work out prices and create a gift list with bite-sized presents that people can purchase online. For example, if you want a garden makeover, a landscape gardener will visit to consult on the design and then draw up a list of items such as decking boards, plants or a water feature, broken down into parts so people can afford to contribute to the overall effect. Or you can just divide up the total cost into varying amounts, so people with different budgets can contribute.

Another good alternative for the couple who has everything is a gift list for your honeymoon. There are companies who will set up gift lists detailing costs of your honeymoon that people can contribute to; for example, a night at a hotel, entry to a museum, dinner overlooking the sea or a helicopter ride. Marianne Rogerson, of HoneyMoney, says: 'Remember to include a wide variety of prices to allow for all budgets. We normally recommend a few gifts in the £100–£150 range and a few in the £20 range, with the majority somewhere in between. Multiple small gifts are good to add to, for example, 10 cocktails at £5 each, as they allow people to mix and match.'

Charity lists

Another option is to have a gift list with donations to charity. The obvious choice for a civil partnership is Stonewall. You set up an account with them and the charity gives you a reference number to pass on to your guests. They, in turn, can make donations by credit card or cheque. Stonewall gives examples of what donations will buy, such as:

- £10 will pay for mailing 20 headteachers with a pack to help them address homophobic bullying.
- £30 will pay for the distribution of 350 postcards as part of an awareness-raising campaign. These will be sent from lesbian and gay adults to their old schools detailing the bullying that they encountered.
- £50 will pay for briefings on discrimination against lesbians and gay men to go to 25 MPs.
- £100 will enable Stonewall to keep a designated Education for All

website running for a week. This will mean that schools can download resources, and children from across the country can anonymously post their views and share experiences.

Other charities that have gift lists are Cancer Research UK (see www.giveincelebration.org) and Oxfam (see www. oxfamunwrapped. com). If you want a green wedding list, visit www.ourgreen weddinglist.com.

If you want to give to a range of charities, you can create a list with the Alternative Wedding List at www.give-it.org.uk. Each charity gives you a range of options at different price brackets, as with the Stonewall example above. The charities include Barnardo's, FARM-Africa, Marie Curie Cancer Care, Samaritans, Terrence Higgins Trust and War on Want.

Thank yous

Remember to keep a list of who gave you what so that you can thank people appropriately. If people bring presents to the reception and you decide to open them there, tuck the labels into the presents as an aide-memoire.

Booking suppliers

If you think of your wedding day as a performance, you need to start booking key characters such as musicians, photographers and florists, to add colour and vibrancy. Whether you want a video crew, a pink Cadillac, or a vicar in a rainbow-coloured sash to bless your union, it's time to indulge your fantasy of your perfect day.

This chapter guides you through what wedding suppliers offer and includes key questions to ask when you are enquiring about their services, as well as ways to save money.

With all suppliers, get everything in writing, draw up a contract and agree a payment schedule, then double-check all arrangements the month before the wedding.

Photographers, DVD/Videographers and wedding websites

When your big day is over, you will want to relive it through the photographs and video recordings. One way to have a lasting record is to upload them on to a website. Whatever you decide on, make sure you choose the best you can afford and people you feel comfortable with.

Photographers

Your ceremony only lasts a day, but the photographs will last a lifetime, so it's worth investing time in finding the right photographer for your big day. You can view examples of many photographers' work on websites, in wedding magazines and at wedding fairs. I would recommend meeting up to three photographers in person to discuss your requirements. They will often visit you in your home, or invite you to their studio. Ask to see a wide range of their work, from weddings to landscapes. If possible, ask to see all the photographs they have taken at a wedding, not just a few shots that they have selected. From a typical wedding, you can expect between 300 and 500 photographs. Ask to see examples of summer and winter weddings. Paul Demuth of Demuth Photography says: 'Anyone with a decent camera can take nice photos outside, but how many can capture the beauty of a candle-lit wedding ceremony without flash or studio lights?'

Ask to see how they present photographs to clients – for example, the quality of their albums, how easy it is to navigate a web gallery. Obtain references and follow them up.

It is important to find a gay-friendly photographer, since they will be recording some very intimate moments, such as your first kiss after signing the civil partnership. If you are not comfortable with your photographer, it will probably show in the photographs. Equally important is their method of working – you are the stars of the show, not them, so they should take their photographs in an unobtrusive manner.

You should also check if they have a professional photographer's insurance policy. This will cover them for theft, damage, accidental loss of equipment, hire of replacement equipment, personal accident and public liability. They should also have contingency plans such as a network of other trusted photographers they can call on in emergencies.

When you contact a photographer for the first time, make sure you run through the list of questions opposite. Be really clear about what you are paying for, since the extras, such as multiple prints, can add up.

Key questions

- What is their pricing structure?
- How long will they spend photographing your wedding?
- Do they offer a guaranteed number of shots?
- What size prints are included in the price?
- Do they provide a web gallery?
- How much do reprints or multiple copies cost?
- How do friends and family order extra copies?
- Are there any hidden extras, such as food, VAT or travel costs?
- What sort of cameras do they use?
- Do they offer a studio session beforehand?
- How long does it take before you see the photos?
- How long does the photographer hold the pictures on file – what if I want to order more years later?
- Is your photographer full-time, or just doing it at weekends for a bit of spare cash?
- Do they have the necessary insurance?

Budgeting for a photographer A photographer will usually charge by the hour, half or full day. Their charges might sound high, but the time they spend with you isn't the only time they'll spend on the photographs. You need to factor in the initial meeting and the development and presentation of the photographs on websites, CDs, or in albums.

> Photographers should treat your day as a special occasion rather than a job. Don't skimp on the budget; it is around a week's worth of work for the photographer when you think of the meetings in advance and the work that takes place after the wedding.
>
> *Becky Kerr, Becker Photography*

Prices will vary according to the time they spend with you, whether you want high resolution photographs that you can print yourself, or whether you pay for the shots you want reproduced. Extras, such as albums and copies of CDs, add up. You may also have to factor in expenses such as travel, parking and accommodation.

If you are on a tight budget, hire a photographer for the ceremony and just for an hour or two at the reception. In any case, think carefully about how long you want the photographer to stay – do you want them to see you dancing wildly in an inebriated state at the end of the evening? You can ask them to leave after the first dance.

It is tempting and a lot cheaper to ask friends or family to take all the photographs, especially as so many people have digital cameras and camcorders these days. However, remember that guests may get distracted by talking to other people, have too much to drink or may not be as experienced as they led you to believe. You will end up paying anyway if you want hard copies of your photographs. See your guests' photographs as a good complement to your official photographer. Don't forget to give your own camera to a guest, so that they can take some shots for you. As an extra, it can be fun to put disposable cameras on tables to get different shots, but remember to ask your attendants to collect them at the end of the day.

Photographic styles at weddings There are different styles of photography for weddings and these mostly fall into two categories. The first is the formal, traditional poses of the couple and family and friends. Ideally, for this you want good lighting and backgrounds either at your venue or outside. It is a good idea to provide the photographer with a list of the combinations of poses you want. The bulk of these are normally taken after you have signed the civil partnership schedule. They could include several shots of the two of you kissing, showing off rings and posing over the registry schedule. And then you might want to include your guests in certain combinations – for example, you with each side of your family, work colleagues, best friends, etc. Make sure you have someone who knows most of your friends and family to co-ordinate this. This way, your guests can be enjoying a much-needed drink after the ceremony and the co-ordinator can collect guests when they are needed for their pose. If you want a large number of formal poses, think about what else your guests can do in the meantime and perhaps lay on some entertainment, such as a magician (especially, if you have a number of children). (See Entertainers, pages 135–140.)

The other style of wedding photography is known as reportage, which is more informal and captures people in different poses as they move about enjoying the day. The photographer blends into the event and takes shots from unusual angles, sometimes when people are least expecting it. This can also be more like a documentary of the day, taking photos of you getting ready, going to the ceremony, the catering being prepared, a row of women's shoes, etc. You can still ask for some formal shots to be included so that you get the best of both worlds, and many people go for this option.

The finish of the photographs There are quite a few decisions to take about the finish of photographs you want – these include special effects. You can decide to have a combination of these effects – for example, the bulk in colour, but some in black-and-white or sepia. Make sure you let your photographer know beforehand.

Options include:

- Colour
- Black-and-white
- Sepia
- Hand tinting – adding a hint of colour to black and white photos
- Digital imaging – where the photographer can make changes to the background, or heaven forbid, touch up the odd crow's feet, using a software package – well, it saves on the Botox.

On the day itself On the actual day, the photographer will inevitably play a large part in the proceedings. They are there to give you a beautiful photographic record of your wedding day and should work unobtrusively. However, if they ask you to look this way or that at any time, try to be accommodating, as they usually have something specific in mind. It's your special day and the photographer probably does this every weekend and is only trying to make sure you look your very best.

It's a good idea to get away from your guests for ten minutes, with the photographer, not only to take private photos, but also to give yourself a little break after the emotion of the ceremony.

After the event Photographers will usually load your photographs onto their website with a password so that you and your guests can choose which ones you want to order. They may also come to your home, or invite you to the studio, to present your photos. You need to decide if you want prints, an album or the images on CD. Check

Top tips

- Put your requirements in writing to the photographer.
- Send the photographer the invitation so they can get a feel for the day.
- Decide if you want your photographer and/or guests to take photographs during the whole ceremony or just at certain points, such as signing the register, and ask the registrar to announce your preference at the beginning of the ceremony.

if these will be at high resolution and if the photographer allows you to make your own prints from them. The cheapest option is to have a CD of high-resolution photographs that you can print yourself, but make sure you don't skimp too much on the quality of the prints. Some photographers don't allow this, as it can reflect badly on their work.

Some photographers will print the best photos in a beautifully bound album, which can be a wonderful souvenir. You can also do this yourself through a company called www.bobbooks.co.uk – you download software to design your book, drop in your digital photographs and then the company prints and binds it into a hardback book.

When you get your estimates keep them in a file or record in the Budget Planner (Table 2 on page 220), then, when you have decided on the best price and supplier, fill in the final column of the planner. Alternatively, use can use the online budget planner.

DVD/Videographers

Having a videographer at your wedding will mean that all those funny moments are captured in sound and vision. You may be so emotional on the day that you can't take it all in. By having a video recording, you can listen later to the speeches and readings again and relive the sense of buzz on the day.

If you have broadband, you can view samples of videographers' work on their websites, or you can ask them to send you DVDs of previous weddings they have recorded. Most will have price packages – find out what they include.

Questions to ask the videographer:

- How long do they film for?
- How many copies of DVDs or videos do they offer?
- How much do extra copies cost?
- How many camera operators and cameras are included in the price?
- What is their turnaround time and do they offer a same-day edit service?
- Do you have to pay a deposit, and when is the final bill payable?

You should meet potential videographers before commissioning them, to check that you feel comfortable. Talk through all your requirements – for example, how many hours you want them to record, if there is anything you don't want captured on camera, etc. Agree with them that you will have a say on the final edit, in case you want anything removed. If possible, ask them to attend a rehearsal of the civil partnership, or at least visit the venue with you so they can work out where they can position themselves.

If you want to capture the vows, readings and speeches, it is best if you and your speakers wear microphones. These can be wireless and discreet. Check how many the videographer supplies and whether these cost extra.

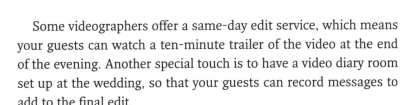

Some videographers offer a same-day edit service, which means your guests can watch a ten-minute trailer of the video at the end of the evening. Another special touch is to have a video diary room set up at the wedding, so that your guests can record messages to add to the final edit.

For something a bit different, you can have a pop video of your big day. Joel Churcher, of Actiondog Productions, says you can hire a music and film production company to make a music video based on your favourite sound tracks and action on the day. 'We can write captions over the film, even have the couple say special words, or repeat their vows over the music, and put it all together in a funky mix on DVD.'

Some companies, such as Weddingstreams, are also now offering live online broadcasts of weddings so that absent friends and family can watch the wedding on their computers. They will film your wedding using up to four camera operators and broadcast it on a password-protected website. Those watching can also use their own webcams to record video messages, which will be played on a big screen at the reception, rather like the old-fashioned telegrams from absent friends. This can be a good way of saving money by not having to invite everyone you know.

Money-saving tip

If you are having evening entertainment, such as a live band or singer, it is worth paying the videographer to film this, but don't bother if you are just having a DJ.

Top tips

- Check samples of videographers' work and look at original testimonials.
- Check with the venue that you are allowed to film, as some places have restrictions and may even charge extra.
- Choose some music to include as background to the video.

Special touches

- Ask your videographer to record messages from your guests.

- To add a bit of history, include some photographs of both of you as children.

- As an introduction, each record a message about why you are having a civil partnership – these can be recorded before the day.

- Ask the videographer to add some of your own or your friends' photographs of the wedding to the DVD.

Wedding websites

This is quite a new idea, but wedding websites can prove very useful throughout the planning of the wedding, as well as providing a permanent record. They are also a source of information for your guests, with links to accommodation, transport options and the gift list. A blog with pictures about proposing, planning the wedding, and what it means to both of you adds another interesting touch.

Some photographers and videographers offer this as an addi-

Things to think about

- What do you want from your website?
- Will you want to update it frequently?
- How many pages do you want?
- How many photographs?
- Do you want other people to be able to add to it?
- Do you want it to be password-protected?

tional service, or you can commission a wedding website designer. The other option is to build it yourself, if you know how.

After the event, it provides an online memory bank of photographs, speeches, music, etc., and guests can add their own memories. If you are worried about security or privacy, make it password-protected.

Andrew Kemp, of web design company Thisonly, advises registering a website domain name as soon as possible. 'You can register a name and "park" it for a while, you don't have to find someone to create a website immediately. Don't pay too much: ".co.uk" names should only cost a few pounds a year, and ".com" names no more than around £10. There are plenty of very expensive options around, so be careful.'

If you find other websites that you like, e-mail the owners and ask who developed their site, or this may be in the small detail at the bottom of the home page.

Once you've found a designer and the price is right, start thinking about the structure of the site – for example, page headings. Talk to the designer about how they might want to receive content. Keep it simple – the best websites are those that are easily navigable and only a click or two away from the information a visitor wants.

When you get your estimates keep them in a file or record in the Budget Planner (see page 200), and then when you have decided on the best price and supplier, fill in the final column of the plan. You can also download the table from www.gay-friendly-wedding-venues.com/budget.

Music – live music, or DJs and recorded music

You need to think about music at the following times during the day (some of these times have specific titles and I have included approximate timings as a guide):

- As people arrive at your ceremony – 'The Prelude' (15 minutes)
- When you walk in – 'The Processional' (2 minutes)
- Set pieces during the ceremony (4 minutes)
- While you sign the register – 'The Interlude' (10 minutes); you may require two pieces here, as it can take a while if people are taking photographs
- As you leave the ceremony – 'The Recessional' (5 minutes)
- As people arrive at the reception (15 minutes)
- During the reception drinks (1 hour)
- During the meal (2 hours)
- After the meal (4 hours)

For each of these times, you need to decide if you want live musicians, a DJ, or whether you prefer to play CDs or downloads on an MP3 player.

Check with the venue if there are any restrictions on having

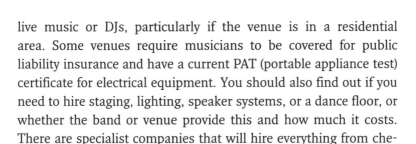

live music or DJs, particularly if the venue is in a residential area. Some venues require musicians to be covered for public liability insurance and have a current PAT (portable appliance test) certificate for electrical equipment. You should also find out if you need to hire staging, lighting, speaker systems, or a dance floor, or whether the band or venue provide this and how much it costs. There are specialist companies that will hire everything from chequered dance floors to karaoke machines.

When you get your estimates keep them on file or record in the Budget Planner (see page 221, or online at www.gay-friendly-wedding-venues.com), then when you have decided on the best price and supplier, fill in the final column of the planner.

Live music

If your budget allows, live music is a great way to add atmosphere to your special day. The price will depend on how many musicians you require, how long you want them to play for, whether they have to learn specific music you've chosen, and how far they have to travel. When you contact a musician, find out what sort of music they play and ask if you can request specific songs or pieces. Most live musicians will have sets that they play at weddings and should be able to provide you with a demo CD.

Paul Rahme, a pianist based in Birmingham, says: 'I usually arrange to meet up with the couple before the occasion and discuss the type of music they like, and any particular songs that bring back strong memories of them together.'

Michelle Falcon, of Bath Spa String Quartet, advises: 'Think about when you want to use live musicians. It is no use blowing £600 on a top-quality string trio during dinner, if you have 250 guests all chattering away loudly.'

When you are choosing music for the reception, a key thing to think about is the noise level of the guests and the acoustics of the

Questions to ask when you first contact musicians

- How long have they been playing together?
- Have they played at weddings before?
- Have they played at your particular venue before?
- Are their charges based on hire time or playing time?
- How long will they play for and how many breaks will they take?
- Are they members of any professional societies?
- Can they provide references?
- Do they have contingency plans for illness, etc?
- Can you hear them play at a live event or receive a demo CD?
- Can you meet up to discuss requirements?
- Can they play recorded music during intervals?

room. Apparently, brass and woodwind instruments tend to cut through background noise better. You also need to check if the musicians need amplification, in which case they will need access to electricity. Michelle says: 'Most classical musicians will play acoustically, unless you specifically ask them to provide amplification.' Check with the venue where bands or musicians usually position themselves. If you want musicians to play outside, make sure they are happy with this and think about what would happen if it rained or was very hot – you could buy or hire a pagoda from a camping shop to give them shelter or shade.

Don't expect classical musicians to play for hours without a break. Four half-hour sets would be the most they will usually play

– that is a lot of music to practice beforehand and the concentration required is enormous.

Paula Smith, from Occasional Harps, says: 'If you are on a tight budget, choose a single instrumentalist who is able to provide the widest range of musical styles.' For example, you could ask them to play classical music during the ceremony, light popular music during the drinks reception and more jazzy numbers during the meal. She says: 'Harpists, pianists/keyboard players and guitarists are ideal, as their instruments are extremely versatile. If you book a melody instrument only (violin, flute, saxophone, etc.), find out whether they use backing tapes. It's best to go for something graceful, stately and calming while you walk into the room and something more exuberant when you walk out.' The processional pieces should be quite short – for example, two minutes – so that you can time your entry and not end up standing around like spare parts. The pianist who played at our ceremony started playing a four-minute piece when the registrar came in to announce the start of the ceremony. She then nodded to two guests standing by the door when she was two minutes away from finishing. This was our cue to walk into the room. Practise walking to a piece of music to see whether it feels natural or awkward. Of course, you can have some fun with the music by playing something unexpected or amusing to make a grand entrance – my friends John and James hired a string quartet and asked them to play the theme tune to *Dynasty* while they walked into the room.

Top tip

If you're on a budget or like the idea of playing your own music, set up a playlist on your MP3 player or record a CD and put it through the venue's PA system (check they have one).

Top tips

- Let musicians know your schedule for the day, so that they can set up and take breaks at appropriate times.
- If you are supplying your musicians with alcohol, make sure they stay sober enough to do a good job for you.

If you want a longer piece, it's often better to have it as a solo during the ceremony, or during the signing of the register, as you get to hear much more of it.

Joy Dey, a soprano soloist, says she is often asked to sing an aria during the signing of the register. She says: 'People often choose one piece – but the signing usually takes a while and then people want photographs, so I recommend two pieces.'

When you are deciding on music for the evening, think about how much variety you want. A band should have a fairly wide repertoire, but they tend to specialise in one genre or era. If you want a mixture of salsa, jazz, rock and soul, for example, you may be better having a DJ.

One good way to compromise is to have a band that can play recorded music through its amplification system when they take breaks. Ian says: 'You need to bear in mind that a band is not a DJ, and so while they can try to accommodate playlists, it is impossible to learn many songs for specific requests.'

Warning

'Some unscrupulous agents haven't even seen some of their bands play, and will literally just go on the Internet to find a band in the same way any couple could do!' says Ian Fellows.

Questions to ask to finalise arrangements

- Until what time does the venue allow live or recorded music?
- How long will they need to set up at the venue?
- What are their space requirements?
- Do they need a power source?
- Do they provide a PA/their own amplification?
- How many chairs will they need?
- Do they need lights?
- Do they expect to be fed and watered?

DJs and recorded music

The main things to look out for when choosing a DJ are a wide range of music (from the 1930s up to the current day), excellent sound and good light effects.

It is important to meet musicians or DJs beforehand to make sure you feel comfortable with them, since they will be creating

- Hire a solo musician for the ceremony – you'll only have to pay them for an hour at the most and you can then play CDs or downloads for the rest of the event.
- See if any friends or family would like to play a tune or two for you.
- To save paying for travel costs, ask the venue or a local church for recommendations of musicians who play locally.
- Contact your nearest university or music college to see if they have students who are willing to perform.

quite a lot of the atmosphere on the day. Find out how long a DJ will play music for and what happens when they take a break. Ask them for specific requests ahead of time to make sure they are available.

If you are producing a playlist, try it out on some friends to see if it is the kind of music that would get them on the dance floor. You also need to time it, so that you have enough songs to last the evening.

If you want a first dance, remember to choose a song that is special for you both – you will probably have a favourite love song or piece of music. Traditionally, the wedding couple dance the first number alone. This filled Laura and I with horror, so we decided to go to salsa lessons in the three months running up to our wedding. It was also a good way to keep fit and quite a fun way to build up to the wedding. If you don't want to do a first dance alone, prime some guest to join you, or ask your mistress or master of ceremonies to announce that you invite everyone who wants to dance to help you start it off.

Money-saving tips

- You may be able to play your CDs or MP3 player through the venue's existing sound system, but try it out in advance and make sure you have all the necessary leads.
- Some cabaret artists, such as drag queens, also double as DJs.

Entertainers

As well as music, you may want to have other forms of entertainment to keep your guests amused. This is particularly useful if there is a lull while official photographs are taken, or if you have a lot of children in the wedding party. It is also a way to enhance the theme of your wedding – for example, if you are having a Vegas-style wedding, set up a casino. Entertainment can also round off the occasion with an amusing cabaret act or spectacular fireworks.

Possibilities include:

- Magicians
- Casino
- Roving artists
- Lookalikes
- Cabaret or drag artist
- Jugglers and acrobats
- Masseurs
- Fireworks
- Crèche facilities

Any entertainer is going to be like a guest at your wedding, so spend some time talking with them before the event to make sure you are comfortable with them.

Agree the fee, start and finish times, any pay for overtime, if necessary, and whether food and breaks are required.

When you get your estimates keep them on file or record in the Budget Planner (on page 221, or online at www.gay-friendly-wedding-venues.com), then when you have decided on the best price and supplier, fill in the final column of the planner.

Magicians

Booking a close-up magician – one who performs in front of individuals, rather than from a stage – for a wedding reception can have real benefits: as well as acting as the perfect ice-breaker, the magician will keep guests entertained during that awkward period while the wedding photographs are being taken. The magician will normally meet and greet guests during the drinks reception, performing while moving from group to group, and then from table to table during the meal (between courses). The tricks can provide a good talking point and help to relax guests, especially if they are sitting with people they haven't met before.

Magician Mandy Davis warns couples to think very carefully about what they expect from a magician. She says people often expect close-up magicians to entertain children, but she suggests that hiring a separate children's entertainer is preferable if that's what you require. 'So often we get guests coming up to us and telling us the children are "out of control", as if we are nursemaids. That's not why we are there – unless you book us solely to entertain children.'

She recommends using a magician either during the reception or the dinner – a magician works best between the courses, not during, as people need to concentrate on their food. 'It's not so important at the desserts and coffee stage – then people are happy to put down their forks and pick a card or hold a coin.' During a three-course meal a magician can comfortably cover 10 tables, 12 at the very most. If you need more than one magician, make sure they work well with each other.

Some magicians also offer souvenirs that guests can take home – for example, balloon models. Others can do cabaret magic if your venue has a stage or other workable area. Make certain that all your guests will be able to see everything from where they are sitting at their tables and that there are no pillars blocking the view.

Top tips

- Magical entertainment is better at the earlier part of the event to break down any awkwardness and before any loud music starts.
- A magician can entertain around 120 people over three hours. If you have more guests, perhaps hire two magicians.
- A magician works best between courses.

Roving artists

Hiring an artist to cut out silhouettes or draw portraits of guests provides a novel experience and can also save on providing favours for your guests. Charles Burns, a roving artist, says: 'I regularly meet people at events who last saw me five or even ten years before. They still have the silhouette I cut for them, usually framed, and can tell me exactly where, when and what the event was! That kind of impact is a wonderful thing to create at an event if you can.'

Caricaturist Rick Coleman says: 'Don't choose your artist on the basis of how many people they can draw in an hour. Accept that you're not going to get everybody drawn, no matter how many hours you've got, or how fast your artist is, so choose an artist for their experience, style and personality.'

Don't waste time with ticketing schemes or lists of people to draw, as this can lead to confusion and disappointment if time runs out. Rick Coleman adds: 'If you choose your artist well they should have the experience to draw as many people as they can, take reasonable breaks at the right times, and know when to "take the Mickey" and when not.'

Lookalikes

Elvis and James Bond lookalikes are very popular at weddings that have a particular theme. Actors roam around the room and cause quite a stir. If you want the occasion to be particularly camp, have Shirley Bassey or Dame Edna lookalikes. If you want to trick your guests into thinking you have high-flying friends, there is a wide range of lookalikes, from Tony Blair to Elizabeth Taylor. If you pick one who is a singer, they will double as a cabaret act. Try to see them in action before you book them, or at least see a demo DVD.

Casino

Hiring a casino is a great idea, especially if you want a Vegas-style wedding. The company will supply roulette wheels, poker tables and gaming machines, and provide a casino manager and croupiers. They will also supply lighting and music to create the right atmosphere. The betting money can also be personalised to mark your civil partnership.

Cabaret/drag artists

If you want some cheeky repartee to liven up your celebrations, why not hire a drag artist to roam among your guests or do an after-dinner act? They will usually tell saucy jokes, sometimes pose as a guest, sing a few songs, change into several outrageous outfits and perform some tricks. When you meet an artist, be very specific about the level of swearing or blue jokes they can use. You should also ensure that there are adequate changing facilities.

Darrell East, also known as Miss Dot Com, says: 'I always ask if the family and other guests know I'll be at their civil partnership.' He suggests displaying his publicity photo at the reception or listing 'Drag Cabaret Show' on the wedding invitations.

> **66** *Surprising a room full of people with a drag queen is never a good idea.* **99** Darrell East

A good drag artist always arrives two hours before going on stages to test sound and lighting equipment. They then put on their

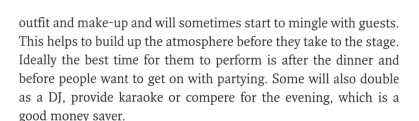

outfit and make-up and will sometimes start to mingle with guests. This helps to build up the atmosphere before they take to the stage. Ideally the best time for them to perform is after the dinner and before people want to get on with partying. Some will also double as a DJ, provide karaoke or compere for the evening, which is a good money saver.

Circus acts

If you want to entertain your guests on a larger scale, you can put on a circus show and provide jugglers, acrobats, fire-eaters or human sculptures. There is an endless choice. You need to allow plenty of space and, if it is to be outside, rely on good weather or have a marquee.

Masseur

To add a bit of luxury to your day and help people relax, you could have a roving masseur. This can be very helpful to soothe the nerves of those guests giving speeches.

Fireworks

Fireworks will make a spectacular end to your special day and can fit in with your theme or colour scheme. You should check that the venue allows fireworks and you need to allow plenty of space – 150 square metres is ideal. Either get a responsible and sober friend to set off the fireworks, or hire a professional company – some will allow you to remotely control them from a distance. I'd strongly recommend hiring professionals since a friend may drink too much, or may not be experienced enough for this hazardous work.

A reputable fireworks company will visit the site and do a risk assessment. You should be able to specify the type of fireworks you require, or ask the company to design the display. Jared Steiner, of

Fireworks Connections, did a display at a civil partnership where the couple requested 'quiet' fireworks, as there were horses nearby. 'We used a combination of quiet fireworks and pyrotechnics and achieved a "rainbow" theme, which fitted with the couple's ceremony.' He advises that a ten-minute display is long enough at a wedding and twenty minutes is the absolute maximum; people can get cold standing outside in their finery.

Crèche facilities

I have been to many a wedding where a child has screamed all the way through the ceremony. If you have lots of children attending your civil partnership, it might be worth investing in crèche facilities – this way the children are entertained and the adults can relax.

When booking a crèche, you need to consider the size of room available – preferably hire a large one with as little furniture as possible. A crèche facility should include toys, books, games, art materials, and sometimes even involve a bouncy castle. For longer periods, a TV or DVD player is useful so that children can watch cartoons or use the TV for PlayStation games.

Andrea Parker, of Scalliwags Mobile Crèche, says people often think about employing a clown to entertain young children: 'This is fine, but they only "appear" for a set length of time and only *entertain* children rather than actually look after them. If a child gets upset or wants the toilet, then there is often no-one to help and an adult has to be called in from the party.'

Once you have contacted various entertainers, fill in the Budget Planner (page 221) with your estimates and then the final, agreed price.

Toastmasters

A good toastmaster will coordinate the event on the day, advise on etiquette, organise your guests and liaise with all the suppliers, thus relieving you of most of the stress of being the host. They can also help in the planning stages since many will have suppliers they have worked with before in the local area.

A toastmaster can be particularly useful if you are not holding your ceremony in a hotel (where a wedding co-ordinator would usually be on hand) – for example, if you are having the ceremony at a registry office and going straight on to a reception venue. While you are tying the knot, the toastmaster will arrive at the venue and liaise with the caterers, florists and photographers and make sure everything is going according to plan.

When you arrive, they will open the door of your vehicle, escort you into the venue and then arrange a line-up to greet guests. This usually consists of parents, the happy couple and sometimes the best men and women. If you want, they can also announce the names of guests arriving.

You should also expect them to liaise with the photographer, make sure the cake has been delivered and is ready to cut, check the decorations, and liaise with the band or musicians – basically sorting out any problems on the day.

A toastmaster will also be the go-between to ensure that the caterers are ready to serve dinner and announce this to guests. They will say grace if you want that, or introduce any member of the clergy attending to perform this task. They will also make announcements – for example, asking people to write in a guest book or use disposable cameras.

After dinner, a toastmaster will act as a compere and introduce speakers, check that the band is ready and announce the first dance. Most toastmasters see this as their final duty.

We hired a toastmaster, Peter York, who sent us a questionnaire asking about timings on the day, who was to propose the toast, the type of meal we were having, names of parents and attendants and if we were presenting them with gifts or presents. This helped us to focus on who to ask and what to buy them (often you present bouquets to the women, but we bought everyone pink hammocks!).

I was very impressed when I was setting up my website that some toastmasters were really keen to embrace civil partnerships. Several said they would campaign within their toastmaster associations for wording to be written that was appropriate for civil partnerships.

There is a useful questions and answers section on toastmaster Gary Picon's website: www.picontoastmaster.co.uk

When you get your estimates keep them on file or record in the Budget Planner (on page 221, or online at www.gay-friendly-wedding-venues.com/budget), then when you have decided on the best price and supplier, fill in the final column of the plan.

Top tips

- Give your toastmaster a full running order for the day, including the mobile phone numbers of suppliers.
- Make sure they have some refreshments.
- Give them at least one person to liaise with among your guests, such as a best man or woman, in case they have questions.
- Most toastmasters will not attend the ceremony, but will focus on the reception.

Celebrants

Although you can't have any religious content at your civil partnership ceremony, you can arrange a blessing afterwards, although not at a registry office. If you are holding the ceremony at a licensed wedding venue and you want the blessing to take place immediately after the civil registration, it all has to be a bit cloak and dagger. The registrar isn't supposed to see the celebrant because they are under strict instructions to make sure it is a civil ceremony, not a religious one. One celebrant told me she had to hide in a side room until a guest gave her the all-clear when the registrar had left.

Some people choose to avoid this complication and have the blessing on a different day or at a separate venue. One vicar I spoke to had her own low-key civil partnership ceremony and then a full-blown church celebration with vows, candles, walking up the aisle, exchanging rings, music, prayers, the whole works. There is nothing illegal about having a blessing or a celebration in a church or other religious setting; it depends on finding a gay-friendly celebrant who is willing to let you use their building. They are also often happy to bless your union outdoors – on the side of a mountain or by a lakeside, and I've even heard of an underwater blessing. There are clergy from the Liberal Catholic Church International, the Open Episcopal Church and the Church of England who are happy to officiate.

You can find gay-friendly celebrants on www.gay-friendly-wedding-venues.com or through the Lesbian and Gay Christian Movement at: www.lgcm.org.uk.

When you meet the celebrant they will give you some ideas for wording and format, although some will only provide these once you have made a firm commitment to use their services. You can also choose your own wording.

Top tips

- If you don't want to organise a blessing on the same day as your civil partnership, you can also get blessings at Gay Pride and Mardi Gras events across the country. You'll usually find a marquee with a number of celebrants willing to offer on-the-spot blessings.
- Don't try to pack too much into the service – sometimes less is more.
- Think about who does what – couples like to ask relatives and friends to act as ushers, light candles, carry the rings, etc. Beware: people can easily be offended if they are left out.

You usually pay a fee for the celebrant's time, which will include travelling time – most are willing to travel UK-wide. You may have to pay extra if you want a planning meeting and preparation of an order of service.

Transport

Your wedding day is a chance to fulfil your fantasy of being driven in style – think pink Cadillac, London bus, horse-drawn carriage, rickshaw, classic American car, or a good old Roller. You don't have to pay for transport for all your guests, but at least think through how people will move between venues, and provide information on travel arrangements. Whatever your choice, these are the times when you may need transport at your gay wedding:

- On the stag or hen night
- To the ceremony – for you and any special guests
- From the ceremony to the reception venue – for you and possibly all your guests
- From the reception to homes or hotels at the end of the wedding – for you and your special guests
- To the airport, etc., for the honeymoon.

Of course, if it's not a great distance, why not walk with your guests from the ceremony to the reception (although keep a taxi number handy in case of sudden downpour).

When you are hiring transport, prices are usually based on an hourly rate and mileage allowance with a rate for extra miles. Some companies also offer packages for the day or half-day. Vintage and classic cars tend to be more expensive because they require a lot of maintenance and are expensive to insure.

Most transport companies will decorate the cars with ribbons and flowers to suit your wedding theme. Often there will be a complimentary bottle of champagne.

If you are on a tight budget, hire a fancy vehicle for one part of the day – for example, between the registry office and the venue, or to drive away from the reception. Remember, you have to be interviewed by the registrar before your ceremony so you'll need to arrive before most of your guests, so a grand arrival might be wasted on a few passers-by, but if it makes you feel special, go for it anyway.

If there is some distance between the two venues you may want to provide a coach or taxis for your guests. If you are hiring ordinary transport, such as a coach, and don't mind about the vehicles not being dressed for a wedding, ask for quotations without mentioning the fact that it's for a wedding. I can almost guarantee the price will be cheaper. People are used to getting themselves from churches to wedding receptions and home again, so don't feel obliged to

provide transport, but make sure your attendants have the telephone numbers of taxi services in case of, for example, a sudden downpour, people getting stuck without a lift, or being too tipsy to drive home.

If you want to arrive in style at your civil partnership, there are some fabulous options. Some companies offer fleets of vehicles such as vintage open-top cars, stretch limousines and cool American classic cars. Or you can hire a classic posh car such as a Bentley Arnage or Rolls Royce Phantom. Once you step inside the car, with its plush leather seats, soft carpet and handcrafted panelling, you feel like the Queen. One company even offers a classic Jaguar with the number plate GAY.

If you don't fancy a car, another option is a horse-drawn carriage. There are various companies offering this service, or you could ask local riding stables for recommendations.

Alternatively, what about a London bus? The old Routemaster

Money-saving tips

- Ask friends or relatives who have an unusual car to provide transport.
- Dress up your own car with a ribbon on the front and bows on the door handles.
- Try something a bit wacky, like turning up on the back of a tractor or motorbike – but be careful it doesn't spoil your outfits.
- Avoid paying for waiting time and just have the vehicle take you from home to the venue, or away from the reception.
- Negotiate a discounted rate with a local taxi company and ask them to provide their best car for you in return for your guests using them at the end of the evening.

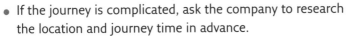

Top tips

- If the journey is complicated, ask the company to research the location and journey time in advance.
- If you want transport for your hen or stag party, negotiate a good deal with whoever is providing transport for your wedding.
- Look in classic car magazines for ideas of transport to fulfil your dreams.
- Put everything in writing and have a contract.
- Buy ribbon from florists or other wedding suppliers specifically to decorate your cars.

buses, with the jump-on entrance at the back, are now hired out around the country and are a good size for wedding parties, often taking up to 80 people. Another fun option in London, if your journey is relatively short, is to hire cycle rickshaws. Or in certain parts of the country you can hire a steam train to add novelty to the occasion.

Some upmarket venues have their own classic cars that you can be driven off in at the end of the reception. Two of our friends did this just to mark the end of the day and have the glamour of travelling in style, even though they were actually staying in the venue (a castle) that night. The chauffeur drove them around for half-an-hour to give them a breather, while guests who weren't staying the night departed. It is a good idea to have a little space to yourselves on your wedding day.

When you get your estimates record them in the Budget Planner (see page 221, or online at www.gay-friendly-weddingvenues.com). Use the final column to record your final, agreed quote.

Questions to ask the car hire company

- Can you see the insurance cover?
- How will the driver be dressed?
- Are ribbons, etc. included in the price?
- What is the fall-back position if there is a problem with the car?
- How long has the company been operating?
- Can you see references?
- Will the vehicle be covering only your wedding that day?
- How many cars does the company own?

Warning

Go for an established, reputable company that is likely to be still trading when your special day comes round. Unfortunately, the mortality rate in car hire companies can be high.

Decorations and floral displays

Decorating the venue is a major part of expressing the style or theme of your wedding. Even if you don't feel you have a strong theme or style, by co-ordinating your flowers, decoration and outfits, you will develop a look for the day. One of the main ways to decorate your venue is by using flowers, and you can also use balloons, drapes, props, candles and lanterns. You are limited only by your imagination and budget.

When you get your estimates keep them on file or record in the Budget Planner (see page 222, or online at www.gay-friendly-wedding-venues.com), then when you have decided on the best price and supplier, fill in the final column of the planner.

Flowers

You can book a floral designer to decorate your wedding venue, or buy your own flowers and ask friends and family to help you with arrangements. If you want to book a floral designer for a summer wedding, you need to start talking to them as soon as possible, since reputable ones are usually very busy over the summer season. Think carefully about how much you want to spend on flowers and where you want them displayed. Choose flowers that are in season to ensure best value for money. The options for displaying flowers are:

For the ceremony:
- Buttonholes
- Corsage – like a broach of flowers, usually for women
- Bouquets
- Posies
- Hall and table displays
- Garlands
- For wedding car

For the reception:
- Top table
- Table centres
- Floating candles with fresh petals
- Pedestal arrangements
- Presentation bouquets
- Cake table decoration

Make a scrapbook of all the ideas you like, such as colours, designs of rooms and photographs of flowers. Also keep a record of things you don't like. If possible, let the florist or a friend who is helping see your outfits, or at least give them an idea of colours. This will help them to design the perfect look for your day.

Make sure you match the flowers to the occasion. Obviously, if you are having a formal affair with morning suits and top hats, you'll want formal arrangements. If you are having a casual free-for-all, choose wild-looking arrangements that look like they've just been put together randomly in a vase. The flowers should also match or complement the rest of your colour scheme.

Most venues have a few florists who they work with regularly and who also know the best way to decorate the space. Don't be afraid to have two or three consultations with florists to get different quotes and ideas. Ask to view their design book so you can see what they have done for other weddings.

It is best to visit the venue with your florist to check what colours will suit the décor. They should also know what would fit the size of the venue – for example, tall vases can be better in rooms with high ceilings.

The first consultation should be a free no-obligation consultation where you discuss everything from the type of flowers through to the styles required for the wedding party and venue. Have a set budget in mind and find out what the florist can do for that sort of price. Be prepared to be flexible, but if your initial ideas turn out to be expensive, a good florist should be able to come up with a few stylish alternatives.

The florist should then provide a written estimate to confirm everything, which will enable you to look at areas where you may like to add or possibly reduce costs.

You should then meet or at least speak to the florist a few weeks before the wedding to confirm any alterations and finalise details.

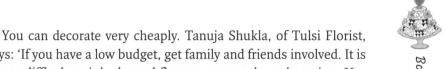

You can decorate very cheaply. Tanuja Shukla, of Tulsi Florist, says: 'If you have a low budget, get family and friends involved. It is not as difficult as it looks and flowers are not the only option. Use candles, which are not very expensive, sprinkle petals on the tables and entwine some ivy or greenery (from a friend's garden) around your candle centrepiece.'

If you want to be really extravagant, decorate with orchids, cala lilies or exotic plants. Or, if you want an expensive look with-

Top tips

- Find out when florists are attending any wedding fairs, so that you can view their work.
- Even if you have a generous budget, set a maximum spend, so that the florist knows their boundaries.
- Make sure flowers are delivered in time, but are not arranged more than a day in advance or they may start to wilt.
- Don't have huge table arrangements that people can't see over or round – they get in the way of conversation and food.
- Be aware of certain flowers, such as lilies, which have pollen that can stain.
- Place your flower decorations on a mirror to give them more depth and reflected light.
- An odd number of the major flower in each arrangement is better than an even number.
- Incorporate fruit or vegetables into your arrangements.
- A single flower in a vase, particularly an orchid, can look stunning.

out costing the earth, Gail Beagrie, of Astounding Surroundings, suggests: 'Go for contemporary, minimalist styles or consider incorporating less expensive flowers in the arrangements.'

She also advises: 'If you're really looking for extravagance and want to adorn everywhere with flowers, take a look at your main photographic areas first, as this is where the money will be well spent and seen for many years to come in your photographs.'

- Before duplicating effort and cost, check whether the venue or registry office have their own floral displays.
- Use flowering plants in attractive pots as a centrepiece – for example, poinsettias, lavender or miniature roses – and then give them away to your guests who played a special role on the day.
- Share the cost of flowers with other couples having ceremonies in the same venue at the same time.
- Fill out your bouquets or arrangements with cheaper flowers, green sprigs, herbs, pine cones, etc.
- If you are doing your own arrangements, buy your flowers from local markets. (If you live near enough and don't mind getting up in the middle of the night, you could go to New Covent Garden Market in Battersea, south London. It is open Monday to Friday 03.00 to 11.00 and on Saturdays from 04.00 to 10.00, but it's best to get there before 06.00. It's a wholesale market, so it is up to individual traders if they want to sell to the public, but if you are going for large quantities they probably won't refuse. There is a small charge for parking.)
- Buy cheap vases from stores, or borrow them from friends.
- Go green and recycle jars and bottles for a centrepiece, or visit local car boot sales and see what's available cheaply.

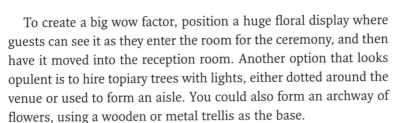
To create a big wow factor, position a huge floral display where guests can see it as they enter the room for the ceremony, and then have it moved into the reception room. Another option that looks opulent is to hire topiary trees with lights, either dotted around the venue or used to form an aisle. You could also form an archway of flowers, using a wooden or metal trellis as the base.

For something unusual, floral designer Toby Roberts suggests incorporating fruit and vegetables in your flower displays – for example, pile apples and berries in a tall glass vase, and then fill with flowers.

Preserving Traditionally, some wedding bouquets are preserved as a keepsake. There are companies that will preserve wedding flowers for you in frames, paperweights, jewellery boxes or in a domed case. Florist Natalie Davey advises: 'Make sure you arrange for the company to collect the bouquet or corsage the day after the wedding, since the flowers need to be as fresh as possible for professional drying or liquid preservation.' She also advises telling your florist that you are planning to have the flowers preserved, as some designs cannot be put into water and so will wilt by the time the flowers are collected.

Flowers to decorate your outfits Traditionally, brides have a bouquet of flowers, which they throw off extravagantly at the end of the day, for the next 'bride to be' to catch. Florist Tanuja Shukla says: 'You can make your own bouquets from a single stem of any flower tied with organza, lace, or ribbon. For something different, you could have a simple garland of flowers entwined around your wrist flowing down to the floor.' She advises taking a needle and tough thread to make a string of flowers, and adding some pearl or diamante beads with a bead tied at either end so the flowers don't drop off the bottom.

For men on a tight budget, if you want a traditional buttonhole, you can buy simple roses or carnations from the local florist, or they will make them up into buttonholes for you. If money is no object, cala lilies look very extravagant as buttonholes.

Other decorations

You need to think about how else you want to decorate the ceremony room, the reception room and any areas guests will walk through, such as the entrance hall, corridors or stairs leading to function rooms. Then there are the table decorations and favours.

To get some ideas, talk to the management at the venue about what is possible and how other people have decorated it for weddings. The venue or your caterer may be able to recommend companies they have worked with before, or they may have props you can use. For example, they probably have table linen, vases, lighting and candlestick holders. If you are getting married in December or early January, the venue may be decorated for Christmas, saving you the trouble. Check if there are any restrictions – for example, some venues don't allow candles, or anything stuck to walls.

Before you go too far, you need to ask the venue how early you can access the room, where decorations can be stored and when they need to be removed. If you or a decorating company need access the day before or hours in advance, you might find you have to pay extra hire charges. If you are doing the decoration yourself, make sure you rope in friends to help – you don't want to be stressed hours before your big moment. Delegate the dismantling of decorations to friends, or if you have suppliers, such as caterers, ask them to oblige – sweeping up confetti at midnight is not how you want to start married life!

The table linen is an important part of the decoration and can set the tone. For example, two strong colours such as black and red can be very dramatic, or pink and white, very soft. The colour and fabric of the chairs can complement your colour scheme. Hire chair covers if you want to co-ordinate or tart up existing chairs.

If you have a strong idea of what you want, draw up a decoration plan, like a map, showing where certain decorations, such as fairy lights, should go and type up a list of what you want on each table.

To create a wow factor, there is a wide range of companies that specialise in decorating rooms for weddings. Some also have props and costumes to enhance the decoration. To give you an idea of how far you could go on the decoration front, how about turning a room into a Vegas-style glitzy venue with red carpet, sparkling diamonds hanging from the ceilings, roaming spotlights, gold lamé chairs, black and red linen, gold candlestick holders and huge displays of red roses and white ostrich feathers?

Fill the favour boxes with chocolate money and scatter the tables with sparkling diamond- and heart-shaped confetti. Hang a scenic backdrop of a Vegas scene, such as a stage of showgirls or the sky-line of Vegas with all the neon signs, on a wall behind the buffet table to set the scene. You can complement all of this decoration with casino tables, waiting staff dressed in costume, and a cake decorated like a poker table.

Some companies specialise in balloon decoration, creating sculptures such as archways made from balloons for your guests to walk through on arrival. They can also produce ceiling displays of enormous exploding balloons that have other smaller balloons inside. As your guests arrive, the large ones are detonated, triggering a shower of balloons.

Top tips

- Check that the venue allows everything you want to use – for example, lighted candles, sparklers, smoke machines, confetti.
- Decorations should enhance your theme, but make sure you don't overdo it.
- If you want unusual items, try a theatrical prop agency.
- Don't forget to decorate buffet tables – some white muslin or tinsel can cover unsightly metal legs.
- If you have dark corners in a room, buy some large willow branches and spray them white or drape fairy lights around them.
- Float candles in water as a table decoration instead of flowers.
- Make sure table decorations aren't too tall and prevent people from seeing over them to talk.
- Look at the architecture of the room. If you have pillars, can they be entwined with ribbons, fairy lights, material, or even plants or flowers?
- If you aren't allowed candles, you can buy battery-operated candles in coloured or frosted glasses, which give a flickering effect.

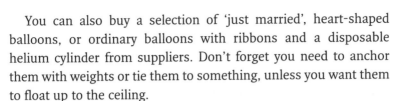

You can also buy a selection of 'just married', heart-shaped balloons, or ordinary balloons with ribbons and a disposable helium cylinder from suppliers. Don't forget you need to anchor them with weights or tie them to something, unless you want them to float up to the ceiling.

If you want to do your own decorating, there are plenty of shops supplying props and wedding paraphernalia. Accessories to decorate a table include soap bubble bottles (allowing your guests to blow bubbles around the room), extra large party poppers, mini sparklers, glitter, petals and other shapes for scattering over the tablecloth. These now come in 'wedding' colours of silver, gold or white. Then there are confetti guns that shoot confetti across the room, and packets of sweets called 'Love Hearts', with your name and date of the wedding or 'just married' printed on them (see www.lovehearts.com).

If you are on a tight budget, it is quite fun to decorate the walls of the reception area, if you're allowed, with something depicting your lives together – for example, photographs or a projection of slides or video clips.

Favours

Traditionally, these were sugar-coated almonds wrapped in organza, for the female guests only, as a keepsake. Nowadays, many couples provide favours for each guest as part of their table setting. They are often sweets and could be anything from chocolates wrapped in rainbow-coloured ribbons to two gingerbread men holding hands. The idea is to see the favours as part of your decoration or theme. They could also be sachets of pot pourri, jokey items or candles. Often the little gifts are put in favour boxes with ribbons on them. These boxes are something your stationer should be able to design in keeping with your other wedding stationery (see page 100), and they can be personalised with your names and the wedding date printed on them. The favours could also go in organza bags, or you can get children's favour boxes decorated with Walt Disney characters. Handmade crackers are a popular option. Other ideas include drinks vouchers if you are having a cash bar, lottery tickets, or trivial pursuit questions about your day or your lives.

See the section on themes (pages 58–60) for more ideas.

When you get your estimates keep them on file or record in the Budget Planner (see page 222, or online at www.gay-friendly-wedding-venues.com), then when you have decided on the best price and supplier, fill in the final column of the planner.

Focusing on you

You will be the centre of attention on your big day, with cameras clicking in your face and family and friends watching your every move. In order to be totally confident and relaxed on the day, you need to make sure you are going to look and feel as fabulous as possible. This chapter guides you through how to choose your outfits, accessories and rings. It also covers preparing mentally and physically for your civil partnership.

Choosing outfits and accessories

When you are considering wedding outfits, there's actually a lot of possibilities to think about. The items include:

- Dresses/suits
- Attendants' clothes
- Tiaras/hats
- Ties/cravats/bow ties
- Waistcoats/cummerbunds
- Lingerie
- Underwear
- Shoes
- Handbags
- Going away outfits
- Coats or shawls
- Jewellery – necklace, earrings, bracelets, cufflinks

When choosing a wedding outfit, one option is to go to traditional wedding outfitters to buy or hire a classic ivory dress or morning suit; undoubtedly the quickest and cheapest option is to hire an outfit – both the cost and time needed increase significantly if you want an outfit made to measure. But there are plenty of designers, dressmakers and tailors who will make a bespoke outfit. You will normally need to allow about six months to have a dress designed – unless you dash off to the Far East (but make sure you don't end up supporting a sweat shop). If you don't want to wear traditional wedding clothes, why not treat yourself to a new suit, dress or fancy outfit to match your theme?

Whatever route you take, make sure you allow plenty of time to find the right outfits and all the accessories. You don't want to end up stressed and buying things in a hurry. And it's not just the main outfit – you might also want to change into something else in the evening and have a going away outfit; there's a lot to think about.

Some gay couples have decided to follow tradition and not see each other's outfits before the big day. This is fine, but make sure you give each other a clue about what you are wearing, so that you don't clash horribly.

You also need to decide if you want other guests to wear traditional wedding outfits such as morning suits or hats. Give people advance notice if this is the case. Even if you are not going down the traditional route, close family and friends often want to know how to co-ordinate with the overall look of the wedding party, so if you want a particular colour scheme, let people know. You don't want mothers of the brides in clashing pink dresses!

When you get your estimates keep them on file or record in the Budget Planner (see page 223, or online at www.gay-friendly-wedding-venues.com). Then, when you have decided on the best price and supplier, fill in the final column of the plan.

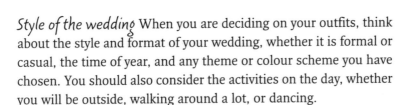

Style of the wedding When you are deciding on your outfits, think about the style and format of your wedding, whether it is formal or casual, the time of year, and any theme or colour scheme you have chosen. You should also consider the activities on the day, whether you will be outside, walking around a lot, or dancing.

Obviously, you can go for traditional white meringues and morning suits, but consider what matches your personality and how comfortable you want to be on the day.

The outfits of both men and women can complement the colours appropriate for the season. In winter, you might want rich burgundy, gold or green. Spring might inspire you to wear yellows, pinks or light blues. Even if you are wearing a dark suit, you may want to pick up seasonal colours in your tie, cravat, waistcoat, or cummerbund. Try to co-ordinate your look with the flowers and room decorations – it will look much better in the photographs.

Complementing outfits One thing that same-sex couples have to think about more than hetties is complementing each other's outfits. You may want to be radically different from each other to show you are individuals, but think about the photographs – some colours look hideous together. Even if the colour match is very subtle and you are just picking out one colour in each other's outfits, it is worth thinking about. Equally, think hard about looking too similar.

Consider having your colours analysed by a specialist. They will look at your skin tone, hair colour and eyes and hold up different swatches of colour to your face to find out what suits you best. Ironically, white is not a good colour on most people, as it washes out your complexion; however, cream is more forgiving. A good colour lifts your face, makes you look healthy and often younger. Apparently, you are wearing the right colour when people say you look well, rather than 'the colour of that shirt is nice'! You might be surprised by some of the colours that are picked out for you. If you don't want to go to a colour specialist together, at least take a photograph of your partner, so that the specialist can select a colour that will complement you both. A colour specialist will also advise on make-up and accessories.

Cross-dressing This could be the occasion when men want to shock and come out dressed in a fabulous meringue outfit, and women want to wear the full tops and tails. You could both do this, or let one fulfil the traditional male and the other the female role. Anything goes. Obviously, you need to find a dressmaker or men's outfitters who are gay-friendly, have suitable changing facilities, and can provide outfits in the right size. The Man Shop in Sussex is happy to fit women for men's clothes, for example. Generally, wedding outfitters will make clothes and shoes to order, so if you can afford it, you'll get exactly what you want. For men who want to dress in women's clothes, there are agencies that will provide wigs, breast forms and large women's shoes, and other accessories to make your outfit as realistic as possible, for example, www. thebreastformstore.co.uk. Birdcage offers a dicreet dressing service and dresses for men, www.bryany.demon.co.uk

Wedding dresses If you are going for the traditional look, it is best to make appointments with bridalwear designers or outfitters. Often this takes a couple of hours, while you are measured and try on different wedding dresses.

Most will have an extensive range of wedding dresses that can be customised to meet your requirements for colour, length, or adjust-ments, such as adding sleeves or straps. Dresses can range from around £150 to thousands of pounds.

You can also go to a bridal dressmaker who will create an outfit from pictures, photographs, drawings, or commercial patterns.

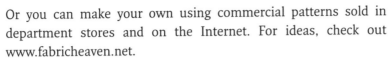

Or you can make your own using commercial patterns sold in department stores and on the Internet. For ideas, check out www.fabricheaven.net.

Jenny Peart, of bridalwear company Ragamuffin, based in Oxfordshire, says: 'We take into account where and when the wedding is and select appropriate outfits. There is not much point having a long train if there is not enough room to display it.'

If you are on a tight budget, think about buying what are known as resale dresses. These are sometimes brand new, worn once, or nearly perfect dresses that were often produced as samples and are a much cheaper option. If you type in resale dresses in search engines, you will find suppliers. One example is www.ragamuffin-bridal.co.uk. Many bridalwear companies will offer payment plans to help you offset the cost over a number of months.

Bridalwear outfitters will often show you how to wear your out-fits with poise and demonstrate how to sit, stand and turn easily, while showing off your dress to best effect.

Retro If you don't want to follow hettie tradition and wear a traditional dress, how about something glamorous from another era, such as a 1920s' flapper dress and feather boa finished off with a long bead necklace and lace-up pumps? Or a double-breasted pinstriped suit, white cravat and spats (shoes)? Retro clothes are easy to pick up on eBay, or in retro and charity shops. In

> 66 *The great thing about civil partnerships is that there aren't any 'rules' or traditions in place. You can make them up as you go along. With this in mind I think brides should remember who they are on their wedding day and remain true to themselves. So often people put on a different personality when they put on their wedding dress.* 99 Melanie Hancox, Ivory Towers Couture

London, there are two areas of retro clothes shops and market stalls – around Spitalfields market and in Covent Garden.

Suits If you both decide to wear suits, this is a great way to co-ordinate your look for the day. You can distinguish between the two of you by the cut and colour of the suit and the accessories, such as ties, bow ties, waistcoats or hankerchiefs. You need to decide which type of suit you want to wear – choose from the traditional morning, lounge suit, or tuxedo. A morning suit consists of a jacket with long tails, a waistcoat and pinstriped trousers, and is usually worn with a white wing-collar shirt and cravat or tie. A top hat and gloves finish off the outfit, or you could hire a matching handkerchief. A lounge suit can be worn with a waistcoat. The classic dinner jacket or tuxedo colours for a wedding are grey and white, but black may be more practical if you want to wear it for other occasions. A cummerbund is usually worn with a dinner jacket and bow tie and sits around the waist. They are often made of silk and come in different colours. It is a good idea to co-ordinate the colour with your bow tie, cravat, or handkerchief.

The cheapest option is to hire a morning suit or tuxedo. Make sure you go for a fitting a few months before the big day and find one that matches your size perfectly. If you want some of your guests to wear morning suits, negotiate a discount with the hire shop. Think through whether you want other guests to wear the same colour suits or tuxedo as you. If you are relying on hiring an outfit, make sure you hire it in advance of the day and always take a back-up set of smart clothes.

When you pick up the suit in the week before the ceremony, check it thoroughly for stains and tears and find out what the policy is on any damage incurred. Shops often offer you insurance against theft, damage or loss, or they may ask you to leave a deposit. And if you are dashing straight off on honeymoon after the ceremony, you also need to delegate the task of taking suits back to the shop.

If you are tempted to buy a morning suit or tuxedo, think about how many times you are likely to wear it again – is it really worth it? If you feel it is worth the cost, ensure you spend time finding one that fits you prefectly.

If you are buying a new lounge suit, make sure it fits well on your shoulders and the sleeves don't droop over your hands. The trouser length should rest on the top of your shoes. Try your suit out sitting, standing and dancing, raise your hands above your head and put your hands in your pockets – these are good ways to check you feel really comfortable in it. Always check the type of fabric it is made from and how good the stitching is. If you want to get your money's worth out of it, think about the style and opt for a classic look rather than the latest fashion. Buy a suit that you can envisage wearing for other occasions. However much you spend, make sure you feel really confident in your new outfit.

Two of our friends, James and John (see page 65), had a very smart civil partnership in a castle and chose to wear morning suits. They felt this was in keeping with the style of the venue. As it was a winter wedding, they picked gold and burgundy for their matching waistcoats and cravats. In terms of accessories, they had tie pins just to add a touch of detail, and black patent shoes. They didn't bother with top hats as they felt these would be more of a hindrance. They invited men and boys in the family to wear morning suits, but distinguished their own outfits by wearing cala lilies in their buttonholes, while the other men had roses. The single stem of the cala lily looked very elegant entwined in gold thread. They also wore upturned collars to emphasise the cravats. John says: 'If you're not used to tying a cravat, get someone else to do it or hire a pre-tied one.'

Attendants' clothes You need to think about attendants: do you want the traditional pageboys, bridesmaids, best men and women to wear outfits to complement your own?

If you want attendants to buy specific outfits that they are unlikely to wear again, the onus is on you to pay for them. If you can't afford to do this, you need to have an honest discussion about whether your attendants can make any contributions. Some attendants will be happy to pay to hire morning suits, for example.

You can also ask people to buy their own clothes if you are not too specific. For example, ask everyone to wear a bit of pink to distinguish them as the best people team. This can also be done through buttonholes for men or corsages for women – flower arrangements that they pin on their outfits.

If you are buying complementary outfits, make sure this is co-ordinated well in advance and find a date when everyone can meet at the chosen outfitters. Make sure your attendants are happy with their outfits, otherwise they won't enjoy the day. Organise well in advance and ensure they communicate with each other – having a unified look will identify the wedding party and make them feel special.

Accessories Choosing the right accessories can set off an outfit and add glamour and panache to your wedding day. Think through from top to toe how you want to create a stunning look for you and your attendants.

Tiaras These are usually made from flexible wire and jewellery, and are available in different shapes, colours and heights. You can buy them off the shelf, or get them made to measure. For the design, select colours or symbols from your theme or outfits. Ideally, the tiaras should be as light as possible, so that their presence is barely felt. Although tiaras are usually flexible and can be adjusted, if you are buying them for your attendants, make sure you have their head sizes.

Hats The obvious option for men is a top hat, which certainly looks good in photographs. However, if money is a bit tight, you could wear tails without a hat since, for most of the day, you probably won't wear it and will be worried about looking after it.

Ensure that any hat is really comfortable and doesn't get on your nerves. You should also consider the effect it will have on your hairstyle when you take it off to eat or dance. Let your guests know if you expect them to wear hats – nowadays few people wear them unless specifically asked to.

Don't forget, you can hire hats as well as buy them. To ensure you get a good match, take your outfit (or at least a swatch) to the shop.

Ties, cravats and bow ties Weddings are a good occasion to try something different, especially if you wear a tie every day for work. Why not put on a cravat or bow tie for a change? If you have the money, splash out on a silk cravat, bow tie, or tie. However, polyester can often look like silk, so this is a way to save on the budget.

Wedding cravats come in pre-tied or self-tie forms. You can wear a regular shirt with a cravat, although some people choose a wing-collar shirt to give the cravat more emphasis. If you are buying or hiring outfits for your attendants, factor this in when you are deciding on the style and cost. If you want pageboys to wear ties or cravats that match, make sure they are available in boys' sizes. You can also buy tie clips to finish off the outfit.

Bow ties can also be pre-tied or self-tie, but there is less choice among self-tie bow ties. Many bow ties have matching cummerbunds and will come in a wide variety of colours. Standard wedding colours for men's accessories are red and ivory.

Jess and Lee dress their dogs

Jess and Lee, two blind women who had their civil partnership in Devon, even bought bow ties for their guide dogs. 'We bought dicky bows for them to match our outfits. Jess wore a beautiful claret and ivory wedding dress with a train, which of course I was not allowed to know anything about before the big day, and I wore a lovely business suit, with shirt and matching tie, to complement Jess's dress. We bought a black and claret bow tie for my dog, Andy, and a claret ribbon on a collar for Jess's dog, Faith.'

Waistcoats Wearing a waistcoat can be a good way of showing your character and individuality, especially if you are wearing a dark suit. You can choose a colourful waistcoat, or one embroidered with jewels or unusual fabric. You may also want close family and friends to wear matching or complementary waistcoats. For that special touch, think about getting a handmade waistcoat.

Lingerie You need to wear lingerie that gives you good support and complements your shape. Depending on what you are wearing, you may need to buy a strapless bra for your dress, or seamless underwear. You'll also want something sexy for your first night of wedded bliss! If you have a bit of a bulge you want to cover up, you may also want to buy a corset. Try to find lingerie to suit your chosen style of dress, such as a vintage lacy corset. A bridalwear designer will be able to advise on suitable lingerie or go to one of the many specialist lingerie shops and sections of department shops.

Underwear To feel loose and cool during the day, you may want to wear boxer shorts. Or, if you are wearing something tight fitting, seamless underwear is a must. If you are wearing a suit, treat yourself to some rich cotton socks that complement the outfit.

Shoes It is sometimes difficult to find shoes that match your outfit perfectly, so bridal outfitters often sell plain silk shoes, which they can dye to complement your outfit, or you can take the shoes to shoe-dying specialists. You can also have shoes made using the fabric of your dress, or even incorporating jewels to match the overall look.

Black patent shoes look very dapper with morning suits or tuxedos. If the soles of shoes are very shiny, try scratching them against stones or rough ground, to avoid slipping all over the place. Make sure you wear in your shoes around the house in the week before your wedding, so you don't end up hobbling on blisters. Also check whether you can dance in your shoes and take some others for the evening, if necessary.

Money-saving tips

- Look for outfits and accessories on www.ebay.co.uk, or in charity shops. There are also second-hand bridalwear shops.
- Hiring wedding outfits saves a lot of money. You can hire wedding dresses as well as suits.
- To make the outfit look more expensive, complement a white shirt and black trousers with a flamboyant waistcoat and cravat.
- Borrow a dress from someone who married recently.
- Combine a holiday in Asia with having an outfit handmade at a fraction of the cost (but make sure it's not a sweat shop).
- If you are skilled enough, make your own outfits, or if not, ask a friend who can.

Handbags and other accessories As well as dyeing shoes, you can also dye handbags to match your outfit. Even if you don't normally carry a handbag, they can be very useful for carrying copies of speeches, tissues and an emergency kit. Another wedding accessory you might want to buy is a garter, which traditionally conceals a sixpence for good luck.

Going away outfits If you are going straight from your reception to your honeymoon, you will need a change of clothes – make sure someone has delivered this to the reception venue. Traditionally, the happy couple changes into a going away outfit and leaves the reception before the end. However, if you are not following this tradition, don't waste money – having an outfit is only really worthwhile if your guests are going to see you 'go away'.

Coats and shawls If there's the possibility that it might be raining or freezing cold on the day, try to find something glamorous to wear over your main outfit. Even a hot day can turn chilly at night, especially if you are going to be standing outside watching fireworks.

Choosing wedding rings

You need to decide if you want to put rings on each other's fingers, as it usually forms a part of the ceremony, symbolising the promise of everlasting love. Of course, if you don't want to exchange rings, or only one of you wants a ring, you can change the wording and format of the ceremony.

If you are having wedding rings, you may want to co-ordinate your engagement ring with your wedding ring, and you can get rings that are shaped to fit with each other. Some jewellers will visit you in your home and give you a free consultation with a range of rings – it saves the hassle of schlepping round the shops. Traditionally, a wedding ring is made of gold, but these days people opt for platinum, white gold, palladium or silver. (For advice on different types of metal, diamonds, etc., see Engagement rings, pages 39–41.)

Your ring is for life, not just for the wedding day, so it's worth spending some time considering how much you want to spend on it and finding one that really suits you.

Once you have chosen a ring, you can decide if you want an inscription incorporated into it. This could be your names, the date of the civil partnership, a short vow or promise to each other.

If you are having traditional ring bearers presenting the rings at your ceremony, consider having ring cushions, rather than waiting while the bearers scrabble around in their pockets. Before you splash out on anything, check if the registrar has cushions or presentation trays. Otherwise, you can buy beautifully decorated ring cushions with satin ribbons to tie on the rings. They can be personalised with the names and date of your wedding.

When you get your estimates keep them on file or record in the Budget Planner (see page 223, or online at www.gay-friendly-wedding-venues.com), and when you have decided on the best price and supplier, fill in the final column of the planner.

Preparing yourself mentally and physically

It's a good idea at least three months before the big day to start looking after yourself mentally and physically, so that you are in good shape, relaxed and feeling gorgeous on your wedding day. There will be many photographs taken of you on the day, so you want to be looking your best. It's better to build up a routine rather than trying anything new too close to the day; for example, if you start a detox diet or have a facial the week before, you might end up all red and blotchy as the toxins seep out of your body. Try to make preparing yourself mentally and physically a fun part of the build-up to your big day and a way of treating yourself.

If you are hoping to lose or even gain weight, you also need to think about the necessity of altering your outfit. If you have already bought it, you may need to find a reputable tailor to adjust the outfit. Book in some time with them at least two weeks before your big day. If you are hiring an outfit or having it made, make sure you discuss this possibility with the outfitters or designer, and conduct your final fitting at least two weeks before the big day to allow for adjustments.

Laura and I started going to salsa dance classes three months before our big day. This combined getting fit with learning a proper dance, so that we could impress our guests. We did sneak in a quick break abroad three weeks before the ceremony to get some colour. We also had a few facials and massages to help us relax.

Looking after yourself could involve any of the following:

Exercise

Try to take at least half-an-hour of exercise every day, such as a brisk walk around your local park or a work-out at the gym. You can build exercise into your working day by getting off the bus one

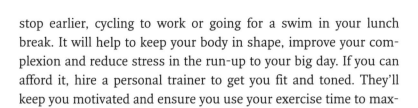

stop earlier, cycling to work or going for a swim in your lunch break. It will help to keep your body in shape, improve your complexion and reduce stress in the run-up to your big day. If you can afford it, hire a personal trainer to get you fit and toned. They'll keep you motivated and ensure you use your exercise time to maximum effect.

Hair and skin

Beauty therapists and hair stylists advise not doing anything radical for your wedding day. Your partner has already fallen in love with you, you don't need to suddenly change your appearance. Obviously, you want to look your best and may have your hair styled on the day, or wear more make-up than usual, but make sure you have a trial run. Find a hairdresser you trust and, if necessary, experiment with new hairstyles well before the ceremony. If you want to try something new, such as a shorter hairstyle, test it out a good few months beforehand so that it can grow out, or be adjusted before the big day. Build up a good routine for hair and skin cleansing and stick to the same products.

If you have the money and would like to follow tradition, offer to pay for hairdos for the bridesmaids and mothers, but if you are on a tight budget, people will probably be happy to pay for their own.

Anne Veck says: 'A good hairdresser's work will last all day, but don't forget to carry a can of hairspray and, if your hair is up, a few grips, just in case.'

Men should think about any changes in facial hair, and try out new shapes for beards or moustaches ahead of time, so it doesn't go disastrously wrong on the day.

Find a good cleanser, toner and moisturiser that suits your skin and build this into your daily regime. Once a week, try a face mask, and once a month treat yourself to a facial.

Massage/relaxation

The stress of planning a wedding can lead to tense muscles, so a good massage or other relaxation techniques can help you to feel calmer. Many people are also nervous about being the centre of attention on their wedding day. Glenn Sontag, of massage company Blue Eye, helps people to develop breathing techniques to overcome nerves. In the months running up to your big day, he advises building something you enjoy into your routine to help you relax. This could be a good work-out at the gym, chanting in the shower or taking time to read the newspaper. Another technique he uses is visualisation – imagining you are in a place that is very relaxing and that makes you happy. When you are feeling stressed, you try to switch yourself into thinking about the happy, relaxed place.

Glenn often works with celebrities just before they go on stage and says these nerves can be similar to the feelings people have just before their civil partnership. 'You have a rush of hormones and emotions. Massage, breathing and visualisation techniques help you relax and enjoy one of the best days of your life.'

- Go to a training school for hairdressers, beauty therapists, masseurs, even dentists, and offer to be a guinea pig – often you get free or cheap treatments.
- If you're having your partnership ceremony in the summer, why not take up running a few months before? Running outside not only improves fitness, but also releases happy endorphins and reduces feelings of stress.

Detoxing

Try to establish a healthier lifestyle, so that your skin glows and your hair shines, by having a bit of a detox a few months before your wedding. Cut down on the booze, buy a juicer and eat more fruit, vegetables and health food such as pulses. There's a wealth of books on detoxing, so have a look through your local bookshop or on Amazon.

Dance classes

This is a good way of keeping fit and preparing for the day of your ceremony. There is a range of gay dance classes in London, from Latin to ballroom – for example, www.salsa-rosada.co.uk offers gay salsa lessons. There has been a resurgence in dance classes since the TV programme *Strictly Come Dancing*, so if you can't find a specifically gay dance class in your area join a hettie one, but insist on dancing together if you want to.

7. Getting down to detail

It's time to map out your detailed plans for the day. I think this is one of the best parts of planning your wedding – involving your family and friends. You need to decide on the order of the ceremony, who you want as speakers and other roles for everyone to play. People usually love to be asked to help and it gives the occasion a great momentum with everyone getting excited about their part in your celebrations. There is also a very practical side to this chapter – ensuring you have thought of everything in detail and delegated tasks, so that you can relax on the day.

Send out invitations

Etiquette has it that you send out invitations at least six weeks in advance; I would say at least three months before is better to allow time for RSVPs a month later, and then it isn't too late to invite other people if you have refusals. You can probably bank on at least ten per cent of people not being able to accept your invitation. However, I wouldn't risk inviting more people than you can accommodate – licensed wedding venues have strict maximum numbers for the ceremony.

Make sure you keep accurate lists of who is invited to which part of the event. You can download invitation management software from the Internet, set up a spreadsheet, or write lists. Whichever route you choose, make sure you record acceptances, refusals, any dietary requirements and other relevant requests, such as disabled access, parking spaces, etc.

When you send out the invitations, don't forget all the information you need to add. Unless it is on the invitation, this can go on a separate sheet tucked in the envelope. Details include:

- Directions by road and public transport
- Parking arrangements
- Dress code
- Local accommodation
- Address for RSVP
- Mobile phone number for emergencies on the day
- Dietary requirements
- Latest date for RSVPs
- Gift list details
- Finally, make it clear if children are invited.

Choose readings, speakers and other roles for friends and family

Think carefully about who you want to ask to read, speak, or take on other roles at your civil partnership. Try to get a balance – involving both sides of your family, old friends and new. You also need to consider which personality types are best suited to different roles – for example, confident people with a sense of humour may prefer to give speeches, whereas more serious people might prefer to give a reading. However, be prepared for the most flamboyant people to suddenly turn all shy on you and say they don't want to give a speech. When you ask people, give them a get out clause. For example, 'we would love you to give a speech, but totally understand if this fills you with dread; we won't be offended, we have other roles that you may want to fulfil.'

Deciding between people and trying not to offend anyone can be quite a minefield. If there is a risk of offending someone, it is best to deal with it before the day. Explain why you have chosen other people, say that you value their friendship and you hope they understand. We tried to involve as many people as possible, asking 12 guests to read out love quotes at the beginning of our ceremony to represent the 12 years we have been together. This only took five minutes, but was a good way to include people from different parts of our lives. We also delegated loads of tasks so that many people had a small part to play that wasn't too onerous – it made them feel involved and left us free from worrying about detail.

Readings

Bear in mind that you can only choose readings and vows that have no religious content. This is the same for straight couples who have a civil wedding, although they can choose to have a wedding in a church, which we cannot. The registry office will give you examples of vows, or you can make up your own. Think about how many speeches or readings you want at the ceremony. You generally have time for two or three readings, depending on their length. If you want to involve more people, you can ask them to stand up and say a short quote or phrase about love.

There isn't a strict limit on how long the ceremony can take, but the registrar will normally expect it to be no longer than 30–40 minutes. Make sure you have enough content to give it substance, but not too much so people start to fidget. If it's in a registry office, there may be another ceremony after yours, so check this out. Read the wording out loud and time it – ours took 12 minutes to read the poems and love quotes, but the ceremony actually lasted half an hour because of the music, exchanging vows, signing the register, and time for photographs. The registrar will have to approve the wording for the ceremony, including any readings or speeches. They will also advise you on the format. For example, our registrar advised us against having a poem at the end as she said it would kill the atmosphere of celebration, after we had signed the register.

Speeches

Traditionally, the father of the bride gives the first speech, followed by the groom and then the best man. The father basically hands over his daughter to the groom with advice about marriage, and then toasts the happy couple. The groom then says thank you and how lucky he is to be joining the family. He also toasts the bridesmaids. The best man replies on behalf of the bridesmaids and then gives a funny speech, usually at the expense of the groom. He toasts the parents of the bride and groom. Well, how sexist is all of that? Thank goodness, we can break with that fuddy-duddy tradition.

If your family is attending, decide if you want a parent to give a speech. If not, handle it sensitively so as not to offend. We had only one parent attending anyway (my mother, who gave a reading), but we asked friends and my cousin to give speeches. Laura and I both gave short speeches, welcoming and thanking guests and saying what the day meant to us. Two of our oldest friends then gave funny speeches and my cousin toasted us. Normally, speeches are after the dinner, but we decided to have them at the reception, partly so we could relax during the meal and also to welcome people to the reception. It also gave the caterers time to prepare upstairs.

Elements you may want to focus on in your speech are:
- Funny stories of you growing up or coming out
- The history of how you met
- Funny or moving stories about your time together since you met

- When you decided to get hitched, the proposal
- Your partner's qualities
- Any advice you've been given about marriage

Try to include some humour, but don't tell jokes about ex-lovers unless you want an instant dissolution!

Think about raising a toast to any absent friends – either people who can't be there or perhaps who have died recently. It is a difficult one to tackle at a wedding because you don't want to upset people by reminding them of grief, but equally it may seem hard-hearted not to. My father had died 18 months earlier, but I would have found it too hard to say anything about him. He knew about our plans for a civil partnership, so Laura covered it by thanking both my parents and saying that she knew my father was excited about us getting married and had been very happy for us.

You should have a list of people to thank and offer any presents to attendants on the day. You can buy specific presents, such as glasses, or cufflinks that say 'best man' on them. You may also want to thank the caterers or other suppliers.

If you have been asked to give a speech at a gay or lesbian couple's wedding, you can start by saying how you know the couple, include anecdotes about them, say why you think they are suited, perhaps throw in a famous quote about love and wish them well. Try to avoid crass gay or lesbian jokes about light bulbs.

There are numerous books and websites giving advice on wedding speeches, some with blanks you can fill in to create a standardised speech, and others that will customise a speech for you. There are also books and websites offering wedding jokes. However, I think it's best if you speak from the heart, rehearse your speech in front of the mirror, or even record it. Use cue cards or, if you can, memorise it. Keep it short, take a few deep breaths before you deliver it, smile and give good eye contact to your audience. If you get any banter from the audience, laugh and if you can't think of anything off the cuff, just say 'Thank you for your contribution', and move on. If a joke doesn't work out, say 'That wasn't meant to be funny', and move on. If you make a mistake, just say, 'I'll try that one again'. Remember, everyone there is rooting for you and wants you to do well. Enjoy the privilege of speaking in front of friends and family at a happy occasion.

For a wide range of types of speeches, visit www.foreverwed. com/speeches/index.html.

Choosing roles for friends and family

Traditionally, a wedding has a best man or woman, chief brides-maid or maid of honour (if they are married), bridesmaids and pageboys. Nominate someone as the key lynchpin on the day, whether this is a best man or woman, wedding co-ordinator, toast-master, or your mother. They should have copies of all the documents listed on page ooo, plenty of cash for taxis or last-minute necessities, and a mobile phone with plenty of juice and credit. Delegate as many tasks as possible to people, so you don't have to worry about anything on the day. People like to feel involved, so don't be afraid to ask.

One vital role to delegate is that of welcoming people – you may be having your meeting with the registrar when guests arrive, so this is important. You may also want people to hand out button-holes, act as ring bearers, be available to check the reception room, liaise with caterers and other suppliers, be a master of ceremonies, and make sure you get home or to your next destination safely. You also need someone to collect any props, such as disposable cameras or decorations, the next day and return any hired clothes.

Andy says, Go for it

Once gay marriage became an option, I realised how special it would be to celebrate my own ten-year relationship with friends and family, and to have the same rights as everyone else.

When we first planned to marry, we both imagined an informal gathering in a bar, with perhaps 30 people. Then you make a list, and realise there are 100 people. Next, you realise you want to feed everyone well, and have a dance. Then you decide that if all those people are coming, it's worth doing something a bit special. And before you know it – you're having a full-on wedding!

To other gay couples thinking of getting married. I would say 'go for it'. If your friends and family are anything like ours, you will be bowled over by how pleased and excited everyone is about it. The planning can have its stressful moments, but get all your close friends involved in it and they will buoy you along all the way. And I'd say go for best men, bridesmaids, matrons of honour, etc. Although it might seem a bit silly, on the day it's really nice having all your close friends with an official role, and something to do towards the day.

Andy May, Canal Boat Builder, London

These are the traditional tasks of a best man or woman:

To look after the rings

To manage the other attendants

To be a witness

To handle any payments necessary on the day

To make a toast to the happy couple

To dance with both partners at the reception

To be responsible for and decorate the couple's transport at the
end of the reception

To look after any belongings or props that you need to take away
at the end or store them

**These are the traditional tasks of chief bridesmaid,
man of honour, call them what you will:**

To touch up any make-up on the day

To oversee the flower arrangements and decorations on the day

To usher guests around on the day

To give a toast after the best man or woman

To keep a list of presents and make sure they are safe

**Traditional tasks of an usher (it is a good idea to have
several ushers):**

To check the ceremony room is ready

To oversee any parking arrangements

To direct people to the ceremony room, toilets, etc.

To hand out order of ceremony sheets

To make sure everyone sits in the right place

To liaise with musicians, photographers, etc.

To show any latecomers to seats

To direct people to the reception

To make sure guests know where the cloakrooms are at
the reception.

Prepare detailed plans and lists for the day

To make sure the day itself goes smoothly, I recommend:

- An overall timetable
- A detailed running order
- An order of day for guests
- An order of ceremony for guests
- Table plan
- Copies of speeches and readings
- List of mobile phone numbers of suppliers and key guests
- Decoration plan.

The overall timetable is a quick reference for you, the suppliers and your attendants. The detailed running order is for suppliers and the lynchpin guests on the day. You may want an order of the day to detail what is happening, so that guests know what to expect after the ceremony. The order of ceremony is to hand out to guests and can be a souvenir of the readings.

Run through the day minute-by-minute to think of every eventuality and prepare contingency plans.

Think about how you are going to enter the ceremony room – do you want key guests to be in a procession with you? Should seats be reserved for key people who are reading, being witnesses, or ring bearers? Do you want music to be played as you enter? Do you want music and photos while you sign the register? What about when you leave – do you want guests to leave first and wait for you to sweep down a staircase with them waiting at the bottom, ready to throw confetti at you? If you are a sportsperson, do you want an arch of people holding, for example, hockey sticks or tennis rackets to walk through? Are you going to have a receiving line at the reception? Think about where you want people to take photographs – is

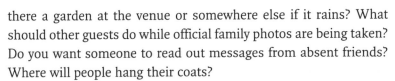

there a garden at the venue or somewhere else if it rains? What should other guests do while official family photos are being taken? Do you want someone to read out messages from absent friends? Where will people hang their coats?

Below are examples of the first three detailed plans – these are what we used for our wedding and give you an illustration of what you need to think about.

However, don't get too stressed if timings go slightly out of kilter; the main thing is that you arrive on time.

Overall timetable

08.00am Wake up – always a good start!

11.00am Drive to Canal Museum to deliver booze and decorations

11.30–12.00 Blow up balloons and store other stuff

12.15pm Check into hotel and have lunch

2.00pm Siesta

2.30pm Bath, make-up, have hair styled and dress

3.55pm Taxi from hotel to registry office, Judd Street

4.00pm Meet photographer, musician and welcoming party

4.15pm Meet with registrar

4.30pm Ceremony at Judd Street

5.30pm Reception at Canal Museum

7.00pm Dinner

8.30pm Live band and dancing

12.00 midnight Taxi back to hotel

Detailed running order

This should include all mobile telephone numbers of any suppliers involved in the day, in case they don't turn up on time.

08.00am Wake up, pack car with clothes for wedding, evening and next day, make-up, jewellery, contact list, speeches, documents, readings, money, presents for attendants, emergency kit, rings, champagne for hotel, tissues, order of ceremony

10.00am Have hair styled

11.00am Drive to Canal Museum with John and James, Pam and Dermot to drop off wine, soft drinks, champagne, vases, flowers, candles and holders, fairy lights, balloons, Ipod and speakers, table plan, change of clothes for evening, presents for attendants

11.30–12.00 Leave Pam and Dermot to do flowers and balloons; show them how we envisage decorations and give them decoration plan as reference. Give John and James copies of readings, tissues, order of ceremony sheets and maps, to hand out to guests

12.15pm Check into hotel and have lunch

2.00pm Siesta

2.30pm Bath, make-up and dress. Anne to do make-up

3.55pm Martin drives us from hotel to registry office. Don't forget speeches, handbags and tissues

4.00pm Meet photographer and have a few photographs taken on stairs before guests arrive. John and James set up ceremony room and help musicians set up. John to co-ordinate best people team

4.15pm Interview with registrar. Best people team greets guests, shows them to the ceremony room and hands out tissues and order of ceremony sheets. Also reserves seats for readers. Photographer to take reportage-style photos.

4.30pm Meanwhile, suppliers to arrive at Canal Museum, caterer to chill drinks, set up nine tables of 10 and buffet, put out flowers, table decorations, two bottles of each colour wine and water per table, party poppers, place settings, table numbers, conversation clues [see under Table plans pages 189–191] and table plan upstairs and set up champagne reception downstairs. Band to set up and do sound checks and put up glitter balls and fairy lights upstairs. Chocolate fountain company to set up downstairs. Toastmaster to liaise with caterers and check decoration.

4.30pm Ceremony at Judd Street Registry Office, Council Chambers

- Nicola and Laura to walk in holding hands to sound of Debussy's *Dr Gradus ad Parnassum* from *Children's Corner Suite*
- Registrar to introduce and conduct ceremony
- Friends to read love quotes
- Nicola's mother to give first reading
- Nicola and Laura to read poems to each other
- John and James to be ring bearers
- Exchange of rings
- Anne to give final reading
- Signing of register – pianist to play Bach Prelude No. 1
- Nicky and Jo to be witnesses
- Guests leave first, to Debussy's *1st Arabesque*
- Guests wait on stairs to greet Nicola and Laura as they come down the staircase

5.00pm Photos of Nicola and Laura and groups shots on marble stairs of Town Hall. Martin to drive our camper van, which he has decorated, to the front steps

5.15pm Martin to drive us to Canal Museum; photos of us getting in camper van. John and James to have taxi number in case it's raining and others need transport

5.30pm Reception at Canal Museum

- Photographer to take reportage-style photographs
- Pam and Dermot to check flower arrangements and decorations
- Laura and Nicola to greet guests, caterers to hand out champagne, guests to help themselves to chocolate fountain with help of operator
- When everyone has arrived, toastmaster to introduce speeches by Laura, Nicola, Mark and Pam and toast from Philip and then everyone to continue mingling.
- Toastmaster to check that caterers are ready and music is organised upstairs
- Caterer to supply plated food for band, toastmaster and photographer

7.00pm Dinner – Toastmaster to ask guests to go upstairs, table plan on wall. Caterer to serve two tables at a time and top-up drinks. Band to play background music on playlists through speakers. Hosts of tables to be responsible for attracting waiters if drinks run out

8.30–9.15pm Band to play. Laura and Nicola take first dance

9.00pm Toastmaster and photographer leave

9.15–9.45pm Dance tunes on band's speakers

9.45–11pm Band to play

11–12.00 midnight Dance tunes on band's speakers

12.00 midnight Taxi back to hotel. Caterers clear up and leave, storing anything in room booked for storage.

Order of day

4.30pm Welcome to Laura and Nicola's civil partnership
Ceremony starts to music by Helen Jeffes

Introduction by registrar
Friends to read love quotes
Reading by Nicola's mother
Promises to each other
Exchange of rings
Reading by Anne
Signing of Civil Partnership Register, music by Helen Jeffes
Music by Helen Jeffes
Followed by:

5.30pm Pink bubbly reception at Canal Museum

7.00pm Dinner at Canal Museum

8.30pm Live music and dancing

12.00 midnight Carriages

Table plans

If you are having a sit-down meal, it is a good idea to have a seating plan. You know all your guests and you can sit people who you think are compatible on the same table. You can either draw the number of tables you have on a sheet of paper and go through your guest list allocating people to tables, or you can use one of the many seating plan software packages available on the Internet. These allow you to input existing guest lists from spreadsheets. You can then specify who should sit together and who should be apart. The software will assign seats for you and you can adjust as necessary. It will also allow you to mark people with dietary requirements and print off guest lists, table plans, place cards and table cards, if you have not had these printed with your other wedding stationery (see pages 100-111).

Start your table plan when you have heard back from all your guests, but be prepared to change it right up to the last week, if people drop out. If you are producing the table plan by hand, it is a good idea to write in the names in pencil until a few days before the big day and then write over them in pen when you are as certain as you can be about who is attending. If you are having the plan printed or are running it off your computer, either leave the final version until the last week or be prepared to make adjustments to it with, for example, sticky labels to cover up names. If you can't wait until the last week and people drop out, let the caterers know of any changes so they can lay the tables appropriately.

If you want the meal to be slightly less formal, you can just allocate a specific table to each guest and not prescribe who they sit next to, or you can have a free for all. At first, Laura and I thought we wouldn't have a seating plan, but we decided we knew who was likely to get on with each other, so we decided to plan it. In fact, as part of the process, we wrote down what we thought people had in common and left what we called conversation clues on each table. This included quirky things, like 'someone on this table plays the trumpet', and 'several of you on this table enjoy photography'. We printed these on the back of the menu cards. We trusted our friends would get on, but every little helps. I remember once being sat next to someone at a wedding because we both had an interest in counselling. Unfortunately, we didn't know this and never got on to the subject.

Traditionally, there is a top table at weddings, which is sometimes a long table, facing into the room of round tables for guests. The happy couple are supposed to sit in the middle of the long table with their families or best people fanning out in order of importance away from them. This always strikes me as very formal – like old dons lined up overseeing the activities of their students. Also having nobody opposite you is not very conducive to good conversation. It can also be a nightmare in terms of family politics. A good way round this is to ask family members to host tables and consider only having best friends on your table, which I think should be the same shape as everyone else's.

We also put families who had children of a similar age on the same tables. We kept couples together, but didn't sit them next to each other since that tends to form a block.

Decoration plan

It is a good idea to draw a plan of the reception room and mark out where you want decorations, how many candles should be on each table, where flowers should go, if anything is hanging from ceilings, where balloons should go, where the DJ or band will be, and where the table plan should be pinned up. Give copies of this to your wedding co-ordinator and anyone responsible for putting out decorations.

Other details

Other options you may want on the day include menu cards, wine lists and table cards to show their numbers – or, for a bit of fun, you may want to give them names, like the 'Francophiles' or 'football fans'.

Another good idea is a guest book, which can be passed around at the dinner for people to write in comments about the day, or wish you well. You could also pass around an instant camera for people to take pictures to stick in the book under their comments. Delegate the task of passing the book around to a specific person, so that it doesn't get stuck on one table.

Make sure you also have copies of speeches and readings in case people forget to bring them. Run off a few copies of the mobile telephone numbers of key people – your suppliers, the venue, taxi numbers, etc. – and give this to your wedding co-ordinator or attendants.

8 Final countdown

By now, everything should be planned to perfection – the venue and suppliers are booked, people have responded to the invitations, you are well into your health and wellbeing routine, and the details of the day are in place. This chapter covers the last few weeks before the big day. Whatever you do, try to keep a cool head, expect that some obstacles will be thrown in your path and see them as a challenge rather than a nightmare – try to see the funny side, if you can, or, if not, buy a punch bag!

You will be feeling excited, nervous and a bit overwhelmed by it all, so focus on exactly what you need and want and don't be afraid to put yourself first above family demands and work pressures. Some companies offer extra time off for employees getting married – you are equally entitled to this by having a civil partnership, so make sure you take it. If you work for yourself or have other commitments, build in plans to take a few days off before the wedding. You have a great excuse to be a prima donna.

Stag dos and hen nights

The concept of hen and stag parties for gay couples strikes me as a bit of an anomaly – the idea of spending a night out with the girls before you marry a girl, or ditto for boys, seems a bit odd. In the hettie world, it was traditionally only for men and was meant to be an initiation ceremony, possibly an opportunity for them to lose their virginity, or the last chance for them to have some fun before they became shackled to their wives. It also often took place the night before the wedding and so it could be a struggle the next day to get the groom sobered up, dressed and to the church on time. When hen parties first started to take place, they were seen as nights in with best girlfriends, where they were showered with silly presents, or swapped make-up tips. Now it is a tradition among straight men and women to have parties, which in some cases have turned into a drunken weekend away or even a longer holiday with your mates. Don't feel pressurised into having a stag or hen night if you don't want to – they can be very expensive and put pressure on your back pocket as well as those of your guests.

However, if you do want a stag do or hen night, here are some ideas to consider:

- Pampering weekend or day at a spa
- Long weekend in a European city
- Night out at a gay club
- Holiday in a traditional gay destination, such as Mykonos or Lesbos
- Party at home for friends and family to meet before the big day
- Trying out a new extreme sport (careful not to get injured!).

As with any of the hettie traditions, you can adapt stag nights or hen parties to suit your taste. Some gay couples, such as Sir Elton John and David Furnish, have chosen to have a joint stag or hen party and seen it as a good way to get friends together before the big day. Often the guests have been both men and women. One man I know had what he called a 'shag night' – halfway between hen and stag. In fact, it was the women in his office and other girlfriends who took him out for a night on the town, bought silly presents (including a blow-up woman), and plied him with martinis. He doesn't remember much, but the blow-up woman remains deflated.

Traditionally, your best man or chief bridesmaid organises the stag or hen party, so if you have assigned such roles to people, check out with them if they are planning such an event. Don't be lured into something you don't want to do, just because you feel obliged to, and be really clear about your boundaries – if you don't want a stripper (or if you do), then say so directly. Be warned, these occasions can involve pranks such as buying huge dildos or other sex toys, tying L-plates to your back, wearing wigs, or dressing up in tutus or tarts' outfits. We can re-write the rulebook. Whatever you do, make sure you have fun.

Top tips

- Talk it over with your partner to see what you both want to do.
- Check with best men or women if they have any plans.
- If someone is organising a party for you, be really clear about what you would and would not enjoy.
- Choose something that friends can afford to do.
- Choose a date a couple of weeks before the big event so you're not hung over on your big day.
- Decide who is paying for drinks ahead of time.
- Or think about having a kitty for drinks so there's no awkward wrangling over money on the night.
- Decide if you want friends and family to attend – make sure you spend it with people who you feel totally comfortable with.
- If necessary, make sure your travel and life insurance covers extreme sports.

A pampering day or weekend serves the dual purpose of enabling you to be with your friends and enhancing your wellbeing before the wedding – have some relaxing treatments such as a massage, facial, steam or mud bath. It's also a good way to help friends get to know each other before the big day. Often spas have days specifically for men or women only.

If you want to break completely with tradition, you could have a romantic night out with each other, revisit places where you first dated, treat yourself to some luxuries and stay in a hotel, just to help you relax in the run-up to the wedding.

If you want a gay-friendly weekend away, pampering yourself or having an adventure, contact www.perfectgayhoneymoons.co.uk. You can find gay-themed trinkets for hen and stag parties at www.pinkandgayweddings.co.uk and www.pinkproducts.co.uk. There are also general websites that specialise in hen and stag parties: www.stag-party.co.uk and www.hen-party.co.uk.

Two weeks to go

Two weeks before the wedding, all the plans should be in place. However, it is a good idea to check arrangements and do the last-minute preparations.

Confirm with suppliers
- Telephone all your suppliers to double-check arrangements.
- Confirm transport arrangements for you and your guests.
- Check with hotels or guest houses that all the accommodation you've requested is still booked.
- If you are hiring clothes, confirm the time when you are picking them up and returning them.
- If you are having a cake, establish who is picking it up, or if it's being delivered and when.

- Check if there is a cake stand and knife at the venue. If not, you can probably borrow one from the caterer.
- Check with the florist to make sure your order is in hand, and finalise delivery arrangements.
- Confirm with any entertainers or musicians their time of arrival, how long you are expecting them to perform, and any last-minute requirements they have.
- Think through any suppliers' bills you need to pay and either pay the supplier in advance if you completely trust them, or allocate someone to pay them on the day. You may need to write cheques for your best man or woman to hand over at the end of the evening, or give them plenty of cash.
- Do a last-minute check of the guest list and confirm final numbers with caterers and the venue. Run through the table plan to check everyone is accounted for and any dietary requirements will be met and are marked on the table plan.

Meet the registrar

Make sure you have an appointment with the registrar at least two weeks before the event. This gives you a chance to run through arrangements and they will also check they are happy with all the readings, vows and choice of music – remember they can't be religious at all. Check that they are supplying flowers for the ceremony table, if it is the council offices, for example. Also ask them to supply water, in case your mouth dries out in the middle of the vows.

Book beauty treatments

Don't do anything radical to your appearance that you haven't tried months before. I heard of someone who had their upper lip waxed four days before and came out in a terrible rash. However, the following are some treatments that should be booked close to the wedding date:

Eyebrows – if you want to pluck them, shape them or dye them, this should be done one week before.

Eyelashes – you may want to have them dyed to give your eyes greater emphasis in the photographs.

Manicure – your fingers are photographed a lot on your wedding day so make sure they're looking good.

The honeymoon preparations

Prepare your clothes for your honeymoon, don't forget swimwear, and if you need to wax anything, book appointments. You also need to sort out any outfits you need for going away on honeymoon or leaving the hotel the next morning. Make sure you have travellers' cheques, currency, insurance, copies of reservations, tickets, travel arrangements, passports, visas, medical information about jabs, allergies, etc, any medication you need, and driving licences or other documentation such as diving qualifications.

Your attendants

Buy and wrap any presents you are giving to the attendants. Hold a rehearsal either at the venue or at home, if possible with attendants or people giving readings or speeches. You can choose to give them presents then or in public at your wedding. Make a list of everyone you need to thank on the day. If you can't hold a rehearsal, make sure all the attendants know what is expected of them. E-mail or post them the detailed running order. Make sure you've allocated someone to hand out buttonholes if you've ordered them. Decide if you are going to display presents and check with the venue if this is possible, then either arrange for someone to take them home, or for the venue to keep them safe.

Allocate people to take back any hire equipment – for example, suits, the cake stand and glasses. If your booze is on a sale or return basis, when do you have to return this to get your money back?

Delegate any last-minute jobs to friends and family, so you have nothing to do except enjoy your ceremony!

Think through a way of making sure you know who gave you which presents, and allocate someone to write a list for you on the day. If you have a gift list with a shop, find out when presents will be delivered to make sure you are back from your honeymoon or at home.

If someone is looking after the rings, make a time to meet with them to hand them over.

Practice

Wear your shoes in to make sure they are comfortable on the day. Pack some plasters in case of blisters.

Practise any first dance you have chosen with your partner.

Rehearse your speech, vows and readings in the mirror and to each other, if you don't mind hearing them first. Try to record them.

Try on your outfit and all the accessories to make sure you are totally comfortable with everything.

One week to go

Things will really start to hot up in the last week – you will probably feel a heady mix of excitement and anxiety. Friends and family will probably be ringing and e-mailing to check how you are, ask final questions and offer last-minute help. You really need to keep your cool in the run-up to the big day. Get early nights, if you can, and look after yourself. Unfortunately, you can't just press a pause button on the rest of life, so be prepared for the unexpected. Before our ceremony, my step-grandmother broke her hip, a friend's house was burgled, it was unusually hot, and the water in our street was turned off while they replaced the Victorian pipes. If you can, take the week, or at least the last few days, off before your civil partnership to allow time for last-minute preparations. Pamper yourself and don't forget to check those lists you prepared in the previous chapter.

For emergencies

Pack an emergency kit of needle and thread; headache, stomachache and indigestion tablets; tissues; tampons; tweezers; scissors; plasters, and any medication you might need. It is advisable to have some cash and a credit card in case of emergencies. Make sure you also have the telephone number of a local taxi company. Top up your mobile phone credit and make sure it's fully charged. If the phone won't go in a handbag or pocket, ask one of your attendants to look after it for you.

If you have anything that helps you to calm down, don't forget to pack it – for example, camomile tea, lavender oil, rescue remedy, or something a bit stronger. However, remember, the registrar will be ascertaining whether you are inebriated or drugged before allowing the ceremony to take place.

If you wear glasses but are wearing contact lenses on the day, make sure someone is looking after your glasses, so that they are available in case your eyes get tired.

Pack your list of the mobile phone numbers for suppliers and key guests, the detailed running order, the overall timetable, the order of day and ceremony sheets for guests, the table plan, copies of speeches and readings, the decoration plan and guest book.

Household matters

If you are having guests back to the house the next day or staying over, sort out enough food, bedding, linen, etc.

Pay any household bills that will be due while you are away on honeymoon and make any arrangements for your home or pets to be looked after. Give your travel itinerary or contact details to anyone responsible for your house or pets.

If you are changing your name by deed poll, inform all your banks, building societies, insurance companies, employer, doctor, dentist, etc.

If you don't want to see each other the night before, work out where you are staying and the different transport arrangements.

The day before

Definitely take the day off work. Deliver your honeymoon luggage or overnight bag to the hotel.

Think through where you need your car – should you leave it at the venue for the morning after the wedding?

Have any last-minute beauty treatments such as a barber's shave, manicure, or eyelash tint.

Put a little bit of Vaseline on the inside of your rings to help them slip on more easily when you place them on each other's fingers.

Eat a meal that will give you a constant release of energy the next day, but nothing that causes bloating or wind – athletes often eat pasta or a steak. Make sure everything is packed and ready. Have an early night.

The day itself

Have a hearty breakfast. Make yourself eat even if you don't feel hungry – it is a long day.

Set aside an hour for deep relaxation.

Have your hair styled. Take any flowers, veils, or tiaras you are incorporating into your style to the hairdressers, or have a hairdresser come to your venue for last-minute styling.

Make-up

Men who don't normally wear make-up may want to consider wearing a little to look better in photographs and videos – look closely at even the most serious male newsreader, and he will be wearing make-up.

Cleanse, tone and moisturise a couple of hours before you put on make-up. Eat before you put on your make-up and just wear a t-shirt or old shirt while you put it on, in case you smudge anything. A mint adjuster is a good idea as it stops your skin from looking red and blotchy – essential for those tearful moments or when the alcohol starts to kick in! When you first put it on, it makes your skin look green, but don't panic, once you've applied even a light foundation it disappears. If you need to conceal any blemishes, deep lines or dark shadows under eyes, add some concealer with a make-up brush. This should be followed by face powder to stop you looking shiny, particularly under the flash of a camera. Before you apply blusher, smile, so that you can see your cheeks clearly, and then apply the blusher in circles, sweeping out towards your ears before you lift the brush from your face.

Use a lip base to create a smooth surface and then outline your lips with a lip pencil. Then add your lipstick and remember to blot it with tissue and check your teeth.

Define your eyebrows with an eyebrow pencil in the direction of hair growth. Apply it lightly in short strokes and try to match your natural colour, or go a bit darker.

Outline your upper and/or lower eyelids with an eyeliner pencil, and then apply your eye shadow. Use a light colour over the whole lid and then a darker colour to accentuate the outside corner of your eye, going no more than a third of the way towards your nose.

Put on your mascara last. If you want it to look really heavy apply it several times, but let it dry between applications. Use an eyelash comb if you want to prevent it from clogging.

To finish off you may want to spray on a fine mist of water over your face to help set your make-up.

Take your time

Allow plenty of time to reach the venue.

You will have to meet the registrar first, so allow time for this.

Take your time when you first walk into the ceremony room for everyone to look at you and for you to take in your surroundings and guests.

Arrange with the photographer to whisk you both away for 10 minutes during the day so that you have a bit of a breather, as everyone will want to talk to you.

Enjoy the day and savour every moment – it will go very fast.

By now you will have planned your day to perfection, so relax and have fun – you deserve it!

Directory of useful resources

Books

Civil Partnerships – The New Law
Authors: Mark Harper, Martin Downs, Katherine Landells
 and Gerald Wilson
Published by Jordan Publishing Limited

Blackstone's Guide to the Civil Partnership Act 2004
Authors: Nichola Gray and Dominic Brazil

Addresses

Deposit of Civil Partnerships
Passport & Documentary Service Group
Consular Directorate
Foreign and Commonwealth Office
Room G35, Old Admiralty Building
London SW1A 2PA
Tel: +44 (20) 7008 0186 (10.00–12.00, Mon–Fri)
www.fco.gov.uk

The Principal Registry of the Family Division
First Avenue House
42–49 High Holborn
London WC1V 6NP
Tel: +44 (0) 7947 6000

Websites

Office of Public Sector Information
For a full copy of the Civil Partnership Act 2004, go to:
www.opsi.gov.uk/ACTS/acts2004/20040033.htm

The Government's Women and Equality Unit
www.womenandequalityunit.gov.uk/lgbt/index.htm

DirectGov
Has produced a guide to civil partnerships outlining rights and responsibilities. Go to:
www.direct.gov.uk/en/RightsAndResponsibilities/DG_10026937

Stonewall
Lobbying organisation for equal rights for gay men, lesbians, bisexuals and transgender people. www.stonewall.org.uk

General Register Office
Go to: in England and Wales:
www.gro.gov.uk/gro/content/ civilpartnerships/index.asp
in Scotland:
www.gro-scotland.gov.uk/regscot/registering-a-civil-partnership-in-scotland.html
and in Northern Ireland:
www.dfpni.gov.uk/civil_partnership_guidance.pdf

UK Lesbian and Gay Immigration Group
www.uklgig.org.uk/Civil%20Partnership.htm

Home Office Immigration and Nationality Directorate
www.ind.homeoffice.gov.uk/applying/generalcaseworking/marriageorregisteringcivilpartne

Imaan
Support group for gay, lesbian, bisexual and transgender Muslims. Go to: www.imaan.org.uk/

Jewish gay and lesbian support group
Go to: www.jglg.org.uk/

Civil Partnership Verse and Music Booklet
A collection of poetry, readings and music. Go to:www. civilceremonies.co.uk/catalog/product_info.php?products_ id=45

Lesbian and Gay Christian Movement
For a small fee, provides names of celebrants and a copy of a book, Equal Rites: Lesbian and Gay Worship, Ceremonies and Celebrations. This will help you plan your blessing service, giving you choices for readings and prayers, etc. Go to: www.lgcm.org.uk

Venues

www.gay-friendly-wedding-venues.com
www.moderncommitments.co.uk
www.pinkweddings.biz

Wedding suppliers

www.gay-friendly-wedding-venues.com
www.pinkproducts.co.uk
www.moderncommitments.co.uk
www.lavenderlifestyles.co.uk
www.thepinkguide.co.uk/
www.pinkandgayweddings.co.uk

Honeymoons, weddings abroad and stag/hen holidays

www.gay-friendly-wedding-venues.com/honeymoons.php
www.gay.com/travel/www.gaytravel.co.uk/
www.gaytoz.com/travel.asp
www.iglta.com/

Acknowledgements

Many thanks to my agent, Isabel Atherton, of www.watsonlittle. com, for helping me to shape the initial idea for the book, finding a publisher and negotiating on my behalf.

Thanks to Jenny Heller and Lizzy Gray of Collins and Barbara Dixon for making the book a reality.

My thanks also to everyone who helped contribute to the book including suppliers on www.gay-friendly-wedding-venues.com and the gay men and lesbians who shared their stories.

Index

A Very Pink Wedding

A Very Pink Wedding

Tables

Table 1: Wedding wish list

Each of you should fill in a table below to decide on the priorities for your wedding. This is to generate an overall idea. Write down your ideas and then give them a mark out of ten to show how important each criterion is for you.

For example, if you definitely want outdoor space, give this a ten. If time of year isn't so important give this a three. This will help you work out what you are prepared to compromise on.

Partner 1

Criteria	Ideas	Rank out of 10
Idea of budget		
Style – intimate/grand		
Ideal number of guests		
Formal/informal		
Traditional/unconventional		
In the UK or abroad		
Location: rural/urban		
Type of venue		
Time of year		
Time of day		
Separate evening party		
Theme		
Colour scheme		
Involvement of family		
Children invited or not		
Use of outdoor space		
Anything unusual		
Other considerations		

Partner 2

Criteria	Ideas	Rank out of 10
Idea of budget		
Style – intimate/grand		
Ideal number of guests		
Formal/informal		
Traditional/unconventional		
In the UK or abroad		
Location: rural/urban		
Type of venue		
Time of year		
Time of day		
Separate evening party		
Theme		
Colour scheme		
Involvement of family		
Children invited or not		
Use of outdoor space		
Anything unusual		
Other considerations		

Table 2: Budget planner

Fill in the following table, allocating a rough idea of how much you would like to spend on each item in the budget column. Once you start getting quotations fill in the estimates column (or keep in a separate file) and then record your final agreed quotation with your chosen supplier in column 4. If you want an interactive version, which keeps a running tally of your costs, go to www.gay-friendly-wedding-venues.com/budget. The items below are in the recommended order of priority given in the 12-month timetable on pages 20-22.

Item	Budget	Who to action	Estimates	Best quote
Engagement party				
Announcement				
Wedding planner				
Venue hire				
ceremony				
reception				
accommodation				
Registrar's fee				
Catering				
canapés				
main meal				
evening buffet				

Item	Budget	Who to action	Estimates	Best quote
reception drinks				
champagne toast				
wine				
soft drinks				
evening bar				
cake				
cake stand and knife				
chocolate fountain				
catering equipment				
ice sculpture				
Stationery				
save the date cards				
invitations				
envelopes				
information for guests				
reply cards				
order of the day				
order of ceremony				
evening invitations				
name cards				
menu cards				

Item	Budget	Who to action	Estimates	Best quote
table plans				
table numbers				
guest book				
favour boxes				
wedding album				
thank you cards				
Insurance				
wedding				
travel				
Legal advice				
Honeymoon				
travel				
accommodation				
spending money				
inoculations				
visas				
Marquee				
Photography				
Video recording				
Wedding website				
Music				

Item	Budget	Who to action	Estimates	Best quote
for ceremony				
during meal				
disco				
live band				
staging and lights				
dance floor				
Toastmaster				
Entertainment				
fireworks				
magician				
kid's entertainment				
caricaturist				
drag queen/king				
other				
Celebrant's fee				
Transport				
stag or hen night				
to ceremony				
to reception venue				
at end of the wedding				
to the airport				

Item	Budget	Who to action	Estimates	Best quote
Fun and frills				
balloons				
wedding favours				
confetti				
disposable cameras				
decoration for room				
Flowers				
For ceremony:				
bouquets				
posies				
hall and table displays				
garlands				
buttonholes				
corsage				
to decorate car				
For reception:				
top table				
table centres				
pedestal arrangement				
presentation bouquet				
cake table				

Item	Budget	Who to action	Estimates	Best quote
Outfits				
dresses				
suits				
shoes				
tiaras/hats				
accessories				
handbags				
top hats				
cummerbunds				
attendants' clothes				
going away clothes				
Jewellery				
engagement rings				
wedding rings				
decorative jewellery				
cufflinks				
necklaces				
Beauty treatments				
manicurist				
hairdresser				
massage				

Item	Budget	Who to action	Estimates	Best quote
facial				
waxing				
barbers				
eyelash or brow tints				
Other				
TOTALS				